JAMES SNOW

The Pivot

A Guide to Moving Forward When the Mission Changes

First published by James Snow 2025

Copyright © 2025 by James Snow

James Snow asserts the moral right to be identified as the author of this work.

Designations used by companies to distinguish their products are often claimed as trademarks. All brand names and product names used in this book and on its cover are trade names, service marks, trademarks and registered trademarks of their respective owners. The publishers and the book are not associated with any product or vendor mentioned in this book. None of the companies referenced within the book have endorsed the book.

First edition

ISBN (paperback): 979-8-9997850-0-8
ISBN (hardcover): 979-8-9997850-2-2

This book was professionally typeset on Reedsy.
Find out more at reedsy.com

This book is dedicated to all those who have held the line – no matter what career field you have chosen. It is dedicated to my wife, children and grandchildren, whose love I do not deserve, but they love me unconditionally any way. Jaime, you are my person and I wouldn't be who or what I am without you and your influence in my life. I love you.

Help me
I'm a rock
And here I will stand
Until the tides turn
And the sun dries my tears.

— Ben "Charlie Safari" Wilson

"It is not the strongest of the species that survives, nor the most intelligent, but the one most responsive to change."

— Charles Darwin

Contents

Preface

For Those Who've Served and Now Wonder What's Next

This book isn't just a guide, it is a lifeline.

While I am going to talk personally here for a moment and address my reasons for writing this, do not think that based on the next paragraphs that this book is only for first responders or military, as these issues I will be discussing carry across all jobs, demographics, people, and places - it affects us all.

I was inspired to write The Pivot because too many good men and women are dying—not just in the line of duty, but after it. Quietly. Alone. Long after the uniform or suit comes off.

For 28.5 years, I served in law enforcement and stood shoulder to shoulder with warriors—first responders, military veterans, dispatchers, medics—people who ran toward what everyone else ran from. The average citizen may experience one or two critical events in their life, depending on the job, but in a 20–30-year career, a law enforcement officer will respond to an estimated 400–600+ critical incidents including fatal vehicle collisions, shootings, suicides, child deaths, domestic violence, mass casualty events, etc. For firefighters with an average career span of 20–25 years, the estimated number of critical incidents is 300–500+, including structure fires with fatalities, vehicle extractions, child drownings, medical emergencies, etc. For EMS/Paramedics with an average career span of 15–20 years the estimated number of critical incidents is 500–1,000+, including cardiac arrests, overdose scenes, traumatic injuries, violent assaults, suicides. In fact, a 2018 study published in the Journal of Emergency Medical Services found that paramedics reported an average of 12–15 critical incidents per month and if you multiply that over 10–20 years, the total can exceed 1,500 traumatic exposures. Add to these the dispatchers who receive all these calls for service and what is worse for them is they are in a dispatch center and many times never get to see the culmination of a call, so they are left wondering if that child lived or died and those add up as well.

A 2017 study in the International Journal of Emergency Mental Health reported that 90% of first responders will experience a traumatic event, and over 30% will develop symptoms of PTSD, compared to around 6.8% in the general population. The Firefighter Behavioral Health Alliance (FBHA) estimates that the average firefighter will witness between 200 and 300 "emotionally disturbing" calls during a 25-year career.

But it is not just the number of incidents, as that doesn't tell the whole story—it's the emotional weight and repeated exposure to these events. When these events stack up without proper processing or support, it leads to what's known as cumulative trauma, which is a major contributor to: depression, sleep disorders, divorce, substance abuse and many times, ultimately suicide.

I've had too many friends believe there was no way out and take their lives, I've seen strong men and women broken by silence and men and women who were once the backbones of entire agencies spiral into despair after retirement. I've had brothers and sisters in service who survived shootouts and deployments, but not the emptiness that followed.

So, I'll say what a lot of others won't because it is not popular to speak out:

We don't lose them because they're weak.

We lose them because we never prepared them for what comes after.

We train for every phase of the job, no matter what the job is, but we don't train for the loss of purpose when the job ends. We don't train for the moment when the phone stops ringing, when no one needs us anymore, when we're not part of the mission and that silence is deafening - especially when piled on top of a lifetime of experiencing people's worst days. For many, it's unbearable.

I've been there myself and nearly been swallowed by the darkness. One of my favorite pod casters, former SEAL Andy Stumpf has a saying he uses frequently, "When you touch war, it touches you back." That can be roughly translated into my words as: when you look into the dark, it sees back into you and I don't care your career, if you see enough bad things, it seeps into you and can take a toll. I have sat in my closet holding a pistol and wondering if my family and everyone wouldn't be better off without me, but they wouldn't be. Neither would yours. It can happen to anyone, no matter how well adjusted you may think you are. While I did not want to turn in my badge, I did not feel as if I was losing a piece of my identity - but I did have a lot of darkness shoved down into a tiny compartment and it was running out of room. I had to learn—slowly, painfully, through work with a counselor—that my value didn't retire when I did, it was waiting to flourish and grow.

That's what this book is about.

The Pivot is here to help you rediscover who you are when the chapter ends and not with motivational fluff and buzz words or shallow advice— but hopefully with honest, hard-earned truth. I've written these pages to help walk with you through the disorientation, the grief, the questions, and ultimately, the rediscovery of purpose on the other side.

If you're reading this and you're in that space—lost, angry, uncertain, feeling like maybe your best days are behind you—I want you to hear me loud and clear:

Your story is not over. You are not finished. You still matter. Do not quit and do not give up, because better times are ahead. There's another mission waiting and it may look different than before because it is quieter, gentler, and more rooted in wisdom than war, but it is no less worthy. You are still needed, you still have work to do, and you do not have to figure it out alone.

Let's begin.

At the end of most chapters, I will introduce you to an individual whom I know personally—ordinary people who are neither celebrities, social media influencers, or public motivational speakers. These are the kinds of men who show up early, stay late, and don't need recognition to do the right thing. They've each worn a uniform of some kind—military, law enforcement, fire, EMS, school counselor, filmmaker, father, wife of an officer — (and some still do) or they've held roles that demanded everything they had and then some and when that first mission ended— when the call signs stopped, or the badge came off, or the war was behind them—they didn't just sit down and fade into the background, they pivoted and they thrived.

I'm proud to call these men and women friends and/or family, having supported some of them through tough times and witnessed their transitions firsthand. Let me tell you—none of them had just one, because that is the thing about life: it doesn't hand you a single mountain to climb, it gives you an entire range. You summit one, only to find another waiting in the distance, but the common thread running through every single one of their stories is this: they didn't stop growing, they didn't stop evolving, and they most certainly did not let the past define their future.

They pivoted—with grit, with humility, with faith and while they didn't always know the next step, they trusted the process and believed in something bigger than themselves—God, family, community. When they didn't have all the answers, they leaned on their tribe and that's a concept you will read about as you go through this book: tribe, community, brotherhood/sisterhood, because no pivot is ever successful in isolation. The strongest men I know are the ones who asked for help when it counted and who stayed connected when everything in them wanted to shut down.

Now, I'm not saying it was easy for them, in fact, every one of them would tell you there were times they doubted if they could make it through and that there were nights they couldn't sleep, days they felt like failures, moments they thought they had nothing left to give. Here is where the rubber meets the road though: they kept going and over time—with effort, discipline, faith, and the support of the people around them—they built new lives. Not lesser lives, not second-best lives, better lives. These men and women aren't just surviving, they are thriving. They have taken what they learned in their first mission and applied it to the second, third, or fourth missions and they are leading, mentoring, building, and serving. They have stepped into roles they never saw coming and do you know what? You can too. It bears repeating, if you're standing at the edge right now—uncertain, maybe even a little afraid— you are not alone. The pivot is part of the journey; it is not a detour. It's a doorway and there is more waiting for you on the other side. Trust me, you are not done with your story - not by a long shot.

—James Snow

Acknowledgments

I have got a lot of people to thank for getting me where I am today.......

To my dad, my first mentor and the one who showed me what it means to be a man and what hard work looks like, you are still my beacon and the one I look to as true north. To my mother, whose love was unconditional, if sometimes overbearing, thank you for choosing me. I love you both.

From the early years, my junior high church counselor (and now brother in law) Russ Groenheim, high school church crew Scott Foster, Mark Trestik, and Neil Golan and our leaders Eric and Misty Spriggs- you all were a part of my life at a pivotal time and I thank you all for the love, support and accountability.

To my oldest and dearest friend of almost 50 years, Greg Messmore - we have had a lifetime of laughs - you have always supported me and been willing to call out shit when you see it. I love you brother.

To the one who fostered my love of reading and English - one of my favorite high school teachers - Mrs. Chris Baron. You took a goof off of a kid and taught him to love reading and writing - and taught him to do it properly. It has served me well - through an almost 30 year career in Law Enforcement where I was routinely praised by supervisors and district attorneys alike for my report writing, to a bachelor's and masters degree, to writing this book - your legacy lives on. Thank you from the bottom of my heart.

To the amazing group of mentors I came up under in law enforcement-the list is long but to list a few notable - Jim Fouste, Rich Bitonti, Ken Madsen, Paul Wing, Donny Mahoney, John Emmens, Rand Padgett, James Marshall, and Justin Snyder - you took a raw kid and molded him into not just a LEO, but a man who could be proud when he looked in the mirror - I thank you all for your mentorship and friendship.

To my Cannonball Memorial Run brothers: Jason, Mark, Kevin, Aram, Churro, and the rest of the Cannonball community - Alex Roy, Ed Bolian, Arne Toman, Charlie Safari, and all the other scofflaws - thank you for your brotherhood and support of all the families of those who have paid the ultimate sacrifice.

To all of my friends and family who have been there for my family and I, thank you - the life I lead is because of the impact and influence you have had in my life.

To those I was lucky enough to lead and to all my students I have taught over the last decade - I hope I did right by you all, and know that I learned more from all of you than I tried to pass on to you. Thank you all for your hard work and dedication.

And finally, even though I mentioned him above, to one of the best leaders I ever worked for who I was fortunate enough to call one of my best friends. The darkness got him before he could figure out the pivot and I think about him and miss him every day. He is the inspiration and spirit behind this book. John, I love you and will never forget you brother. Rest in Peace.

James Snow, July 31, 2025

Introduction

Change Is Inevitable—But So Is Growth

Life is an ever-changing journey, and if there is one thing I have learned over my 57 years (as of the writing of this book), it is that change is not optional. It does not wait for your permission, and it rarely shows up on schedule. It barges in—sometimes subtly, sometimes like a freight train—and it forces you to pay attention. It does not care if you are comfortable, and it certainly does not care if you had a five-year plan or if everything was going just fine. Whether it is a career shift you did not see coming, the loss of someone you love, the moment your body starts to betray you, or a quiet realization that what once fulfilled you no longer does—change arrives, and when it does, it demands a response.

Some changes we choose, while others are oftentimes thrust upon us, and while some are slow and creeping like the erosion of interest in a job you once loved, others are sudden—a diagnosis, a phone call, a closed door. No matter the form it takes, change reveals something essential about who we are and how we respond when things no longer go according to plan.

I will put this out there right in the beginning and make it a stand-alone thought – while you may not always be responsible for the things that happen to you, you are 100 percent responsible for how you react to those things.

I wore a badge for 28.5 years and people do not call 911 to share what a great day they are having. They call because they are having the worst day of their lives and I have spent more time than I care to think about with people suffering the worst times of their lives. I have been in rooms where the air felt thick with loss. I have sat at kitchen tables with people who just got news they could not wrap their minds around – that a loved one was not coming home. And I have faced my own mirrors— retirement, injury, identity, what comes next and what I know for sure is this: our reaction to change defines our trajectory far more than the change itself.

This book is about the pivot—what it means, when it is time, and how to step into it with purpose. Read this next part slowly and carefully because it is the basis for all that comes after - change is not the enemy, it is the invitation. The pivot is not failure or defeat; it is often the smartest, strongest, most faithful thing you can do for yourself and those around you. To pivot well means to trust that you are not finished and to realize that your story still has chapters left to be written and that the life you have built—even if parts of it are falling apart—still holds the bones of something meaningful. Remember this: the new version of you waiting on the other side of the pivot might be more whole, more honest, and freer than anything that came before.

The Trap of Standing Still

We live in a world that prizes certainty with catch phrases like "Stick it out," "Finish what you started" or "Do not quit." And while there's value in commitment—God knows I have drilled that into recruits and tried to model it in my own career—there is certainly a line between perseverance and stagnation.

Sometimes we keep pushing forward in the wrong direction simply because we do not want to admit we need a new one. We tell ourselves, "I've come this far," as if distance alone is reason enough to keep going, but the sunk cost fallacy does not serve your growth. Instead, it traps you and keeps you locked into roles, routines, and relationships that no longer fit you or serve you.

Standing still always seems to feel safer, because "The devil you know is better than the one you don't" right? What we fail to realize in those moments is that safety is not always the same as alignment and over time, what once felt like stability can start to feel like a prison. Your body knows, your spirit knows, and before long you start to feel that restlessness, that hum of discomfort just beneath the surface. That knocking is your soul asking for something new and we now must figure out what to do with that discomfort?

That is where the pivot comes in.

What Is the Pivot, really?

The pivot is the conscious, intentional decision to change direction when life—either through circumstance or internal calling—tells you it is time. That is it. It is not some crazy existential thing, it is just realizing it is time for a change.

It is not about throwing everything away, it is not reckless, it is not quitting - it is a realignment or a re-centering. It is deciding that you are not going to sleepwalk through a life that no longer feels like yours. The pivot can look like changing careers in midlife, retiring from a job that used to define you, ending a toxic friendship or setting a boundary you should have drawn years ago, or even downsizing, relocating, recommitting to your health, or choosing faith after years of skepticism.

With these things in mind, at its heart the pivot is an act of courage because it means letting go of certainty and being willing to ask hard questions like: Is this still working for me? Who am I now? What do I want next?

These are not questions you can answer overnight, and this book does not pretend to have one-size-fits-all solutions. What I offer here are stories, tools, and reflections from my life and the lives of others who have wrestled through transition, faced their fears, and stepped into something new to change their lives – not only for the good of themselves, but for their family and loved ones.

Why This Matters Now

We live in a world full of pressures. Pressure to know who you are by 25, to be successful, to have a picture-perfect marriage, to never fail, or to never change your mind. How many of you had someone ask you as a kid, "What do you want to be when you grow up?" I bet most of you would raise your hand - but what kid knows that? Maybe a better question would be, "What are you passionate about?" With all that is going on in the world today, due to these pressures, many end up in spots they didn't want to be - or they did, but time and circumstances have changed. Let me tell you something, I have met some of the wisest, strongest people in the world, and not one of them got through life without pivoting and while some of them pivoted out of necessity, others pivoted out of conviction. The one thing I can say from talking to these people is that the pivot always brought them closer to their real selves – provided they were honest with themselves.

In law enforcement, we train constantly for the unknown and we rehearse how to respond under pressure in the worst of circumstances. The other side of that coin however – and it is in every field – is that most of us are not trained to pivot in real life. No one teaches you how to leave a calling that has expired, no one teaches you how to retire from a job that became your identity, and no one teaches you how to start over at 45 or 60 or beyond.

That is why this book exists. As I looked at my own pivot in retiring (after many in life that I didn't have a word for at the time), I realized I wanted to help give others the ability to understand what you are experiencing, to give you a language for what you are feeling, to give you permission to pivot (if you felt you needed it), and to walk with you through the discomfort and toward the purpose waiting on the other side of your pivot.

What You Can Expect

Throughout this book, we will explore the mindset and skills that allow people to navigate transitions with strength. Each chapter is grounded in real stories, practical wisdom, and the core belief that change, while uncomfortable, is not something to fear—but to work with.

We will cover things like:

- How to recognize the signs it is time to pivot
- Letting go of ego and old identities
- Finding a new purpose after retirement or burnout
- The emotional and mental tools to deal with setbacks
- Creating space for your faith in the middle of uncertainty
- Building a life that reflects your values, not just your résumé

We will talk about legacy, failure, leadership, and we will talk about grace—because you will need a lot of it. You will hear from people who have lived through unimaginable losses and still found a new way forward, from men and women who let go of who they were supposed to be and stepped into who they were called to be and through it all, you will be invited to ask one simple but life-altering question: What if the change you are facing is not the end—but the beginning of your most meaningful chapter yet?

A Personal Note Before We Begin

I did not write this because I had it all figured out – not even close. I wrote this because I have lived it—and I am still living it and learning from it. I have pivoted from active duty to retirement, from law enforcement to woodworking, from living for the mission to redefining the mission, from being basically "empty nesters" to being a parent again and raising our granddaughter and through it all, I have found that the pivot does not just change your direction—it changes you in fundamental ways that can be quite uncomfortable at times - it refines you, it humbles you, and it ALWAYS has a way of reminding you that you are not in control—but you are still capable of choosing.

So, if you are here and you have read this far, and you are at the edge of something new, wondering if it is too late or too risky or too unclear—I want to tell you this: you are right on time and you have the universe's permission to pivot.

Let's get to work.

I

Part One

Recognizing the Need for Change.

1

1. Excellence Matters — How You Do Anything Is How You Do Everything

To start off, before we get into the meat and potatoes of the pivot, I want to talk about the mindset you should go into a pivot with – EXCELLENCE MATTERS. I would like to share a quote with you from one of the greatest basketball coaches of all time – the incomparable Bobby Knight from the University of Indiana, who said – almost everyone has the will to win, but very few people have the will to PREPARE to win. Excellence Matters, so fail forward and decide to do your best because when it comes to standards, it is not what you preach – it is what you tolerate – and what you tolerate, you condone.

My father was a worker – a doer, and still is to this day at 88 years of age. He never was a head in the clouds dreamer and he did not wait for things to come to him. He taught me from as far back as I can remember the importance of hard work, critical thinking, and getting the job done. I do not know how many time I heard "If it is worth doing, it is worth doing right."

When I was about ten years old, my dad added on a large family room to the back of our house, and as was his style, he did the job himself. As a boy, I wanted to do everything with my dad, as he was my hero and he could do anything. So, without reservation, I offered to help and was given the job of hand nailing off the paneling to go under the siding. I was great at nailing off that siding until it got to the bottom and I had to bend over to pound in the nails.... well, as you can imagine, I bent every single nail at the bottom, and then just left them, because who was going to see it? As I was just about done, out came my dad, and asked about all the bent nails. I explained that they were hard to nail in straight when I was bending over and no one would ever know because they would be covered by the siding. He looked at me with that quiet look he had and softly said, "yes, but you will know they are there and that they are wrong." He had me pull every one of those nails and do it right and that lesson has stuck with me my whole life. Even today when I am at there house in the backyard and I look at that addition, I am reminded of that story and have a bit of pride because I know they are all nailed straight and flush.

To this day, when I think of excellence and perseverance, I think of my dad and I truly believe a hard work ethic paired with a desire to do things right is indispensable. Without it, the odds go down significantly that you will finish what you start - but a dependable, energetic, and determined work ethic greatly increases your chances at success at any endeavor and in any field.

To my point, how you do anything is how you do everything. I have seen excellence up close, and I have seen the cost of its absence. In crash investigations, it is often the tiniest detail that breaks the case open—a fragment of paint on a jacket, a skid mark that does not line up with a vehicle's reported speed. In one hit-and-run, it was a gold Toyota emblem (the gold was a special edition) that led us to the suspect. A detail most people would not even think to look for. But we were trained to expect more from ourselves, to pay attention to details, to look again, and to follow up.

That level of precision does not come from ego or perfectionism; it comes from a place of love. A love for the craft and a love for the people we serve. It is a love for the future we are shaping with every choice we make and I think that is what most people get wrong about excellence. They think it is for the spotlight or to say, "hey, look at me" or that is about competing or outperforming the guy next to you. But it is not, it is about how you carry yourself when no one is watching.

Good Is the Enemy of Great

One of the most dangerous places to get stuck is in the land of "good enough" because good isn't painful enough to force change, but it's comfortable enough to lull you into staying put. You tell yourself, "I can live with this, it's not that bad," and before you know it, years have slipped by.

The problem with good is that it tricks you into thinking you don't need to pivot because you have a decent job, a decent life, and maybe even some decent goals but decent isn't what you were built for. Nobody remembers the people who settled for "good enough," because they never pushed themselves far enough to become something remarkable. Good is a plateau, and great is a climb. The climb isn't easy, because it demands discomfort, risk, and the guts to let go of safe ground. Ask yourself this: are you staying in a job, relationship, or routine because it's "fine?" Are you hiding from the climb because it feels scary or uncertain? And what would "great" even look like if you stopped settling?

11

If you're honest with yourself, the difference between good and great is often just one decision away—one move that shakes you out of autopilot and forces you to grow because the pivot—that moment in life where you decide to change directions—is not when you lower the bar, it is when you raise it. When everything is in flux and seems to be spiraling out of control and when you are stepping into the unknown, it is excellence that is the thing that roots you. It is not about where you are or what title you carry, it is about who you are and even more than that, it is about who you are becoming. I have seen people pivot careers, relationships, entire lifestyles and some people start over with their heads down, just trying to make it through, while others approach the same shift with precision, pride, and clarity. Guess which ones come out stronger?

I remember talking to a deputy who had transitioned out of law enforcement into the private sector. His job title changed, his uniform changed, but his habits did not. He was still the first one in and the last one out and was still the guy who prepared twice as much as he needed to for whatever task he had in front of him. When I asked him why, he just shrugged and said, "It is just who I am." Excellence had become part of his DNA.

But let's be real here—excellence has enemies. People will not always understand it and they will mistake your standards for arrogance, call you obsessive, say you are trying too hard, or that you are trying to kiss up to the bosses. Let them talk. One of my first jobs was at Lucky Store's (a California grocery chain in the 80's) as a box boy (grocery bagger, courtesy clerk, or whatever you want to call it) and a part of our job duties was getting the shopping carts out of the parking lot. As was my dad's way, he told me before I started that when I was out getting the carts I should always run and get them and anytime I was coming into the store, to bring some with me. Lo and behold, on my very first day I had several other box boys/girls come up to me and tell me to stop running because it was making them look bad.

As in the anecdote above, most of the resistance you are going to meet comes from people who have made peace with mediocrity. Your effort reminds them of what they gave up on and that can be hard for them to look at, but here is the thing—excellence is contagious. It lifts the people around you, even if they never say a word. I have had deputies come back years later to tell me they started investigating traffic collisions in the same order and manner I did because it was thorough and I never missed anything (even though I sometimes did). I did not even know they noticed. But they did. We are always leaving a trail and someone is always watching, so remember that excellence creates a ripple that keeps going, far beyond what we see. Remember, excellence is not about where you start, it is about how you carry yourself on day one and everyday thereafter.

I should pause here and say this: excellence is not taking yourself to burnout and it is not running yourself into the ground, as that kind of martyrdom does not help anyone. Trust me when I say, I have worn that badge too—the one that says first one in, last one out, no time off, always the first to volunteer and I know what it costs. It is not sustainable. True excellence includes rest, boundaries, and saying no to things that do not align with your mission. Excellence is not about being everywhere and being everything to everyone - but it is about being fully present where you are.

One more important thing to note, there is humility in excellence and we will talk about ego in a later chapter, but just remember this: real excellence does not puff its chest or demand attention. It is quiet and steady because it knows all the early mornings, the failures, the doubt, and the days you almost gave up to to get to where you are.

Excellence is not just for careers or work, it is also about how you carry your relationships too. I have seen marriages fall apart not because of betrayal or major conflict, but because of neglect, because one or both partners stopped showing up with intention. Excellence in relationships is remembering important dates, listening when it would be easier to zone out, choosing patience when frustration rises, apologizing first, and being consistent even when life is messy. And remember, this is not easy. I still struggle with this all the time as life gets busy and you get caught up......remember to try and be purposeful about it, because one of the most courageous things you can do is bring excellence into your personal life—your parenting, your friendships, your faith, and your health - because that is where it really counts. The world might not see it. But your kids will. Your spouse will. You will.

So, this is what I want you to carry into your pivot and keep in the back of your mind as you read the following chapters. Excellence. Not for praise or for competition, but because it is who you are, and if it is not who you are yet, it can be. Start small - make your bed, write the follow-up email you have been putting off, take pride in how you speak, show up early, prepare well, listen deeply, and honor your word. How you do these things adds up, and the pivot is your proving ground and it is your chance to build OR rebuild with intention and to become someone you respect when you look in the mirror at the end of the day. This matters more than anything else because the truth is, the pivot is not just about changing direction, it is about changing who you are in the process.

And excellence? It is the foundation. It is the anchor. It is the difference between simply surviving the change and thriving within it. So, carry it with you into the next job, the next relationship, but most importantly - into the next version of yourself.

Because how you do anything is how you do everything.

Real Life Example: My Dad, James Russell Snow (Sr.)

Since I mention him here in the first chapter, I am going to use him as the first pivot example of someone in the real world that has probably had more struggles and pivots than most today.

My dad was born in 1937 in Lamar, Missouri and grew up right at the end of the great depression. He did not have indoor plumbing until he was about 10 years old. His father was an alcoholic who sold farm machinery, but drank most of his paycheck away, leaving his mom to be the one who ran the household. She was a loving, strong woman who made sure her children were taken care of, but it was still a rough childhood – although he knew no better, so it worked.

After high school, and summers digging ditches, Pops knew that there was not a lot of job opportunities in Lamar, so knowing that one of his best friends was working for Boeing in Witchita, Kansas, he headed there. Upon arriving, Pops found a phone booth (if you are too young to know what this is, ask your parents), and call his friend Lynn and told him he was in Witchita and needed a job. Lynn took down the phone booth number, talked to his supervisor and the supervisor called my dad in the phone booth and asked him if he had taken a "descriptive geometry" class, which he had. He told the supervisor he had and was directed to go to the hiring office in downtown Witchita and boom, he had his first job in the Aerospace industry in August of 1957.

While working at Boeing, pops met my mom and they began dating. In

March of 1959, while working at Boeing building the B-52 bomber, he was called up for his Army physical, which was a precursor to being drafted. He did not want to spend the next years in the army because he wanted to get married, so he went and enlisted in the Kansas National Guard. At the time by joining the guard, he would do six months of active duty followed by five and a half years of reserve time. During that time, he was transferred to Fort Ord in Northern California and his fiancée' (my mom) went to live with her sister in Phoenix, Arizona. After being discharged from Fort Ord from active duty, he traveled to Van Nuys, CA where his brother Bill was living. He borrowed Bill's car and drove to Phoenix to pick up my mom and while they were there in Phoenix, they got married and returned to California.

They looked at all the options and decided that due to there not being enough aerospace businesses in Wichita (my mom's hometown), they decided to stay in California as it was booming and more aerospace companies were opening on the west coast. This led him to believe it would be easier to find a job. Back then, there was no indeed.com or internet, so job hunting was a matter of looking in the newspaper (again, ask your parents) or just knocking on doors. Pops interviewed with the Collins Radio company, and was asked if he would move to Newport Beach for the job. Dad said yes and got the job, after which he went to their 110 dollar a month apartment and looked at a Thomas Guide (ask your parents) to discover where Newport Beach was and after 6 months, he and my mom moved to Costa Mesa.

In the mid 60's, my mom gave birth to my older sister and my Dad went back to working in aerospace at McDonnell Douglas. When my mom was told she could not have anymore children, they decided to adopt and that is where I came into the picture. I was adopted shortly after my birth in 1968 and then my mom found out she was pregnant with my younger sister - talk about a pivot! They then purchased their house in Fountain Valley - my childhood home - and where they still live today after over 67 years married.

My dad then went to work for the Bechtel Power Corporation and was there until they decided to move operations east and he was told he would have to move. As he did not want to uproot his family, he took the lay off and the pivot was on again. Here is where relationship building and work ethic come in, as a friend and former coworker was able to help get him hired on at McDonnell Douglas again. It was eventually bought out by Boeing and my dad stayed and worked there until he retired at 79 years of age to care for my ailing mom. Another pivot at 79 - not to travel the world, but to care for the woman he loves. He is now 88 and has taken up gardening and is learning how to play guitar and soon the piano as well, and he is still caring for my mom.

They say don't meet your heroes because you will be disappointed - but I wholeheartedly disagree with that assessment because not only did I get to meet him, I was raised by him. To listen to his history as I wrote this book and think of all the pivots he has made in life is a bit mind boggling for me. But he is stoic about it and his usual humble self downplays it as just doing what he had to do. But I will tell you, my dad is an example to everyone that what happens to you doesn't define you - it is how you pivot and respond to it that matters. He taught me most of the tenets you are going to read about in this book through living them and setting example for me to follow.

This is not a magic formula - he would tell you that if a small town boy from poverty and a hard upbringing can pivot and thrive - you can too, so get after it because hard work wins. Hard. Work. Wins.

📓 Reflection & Action

1. What part of this chapter resonated with you most? Why?

2. What is one action you can take this week to apply a principle discussed here?
3. Are there any habits or beliefs you need to let go of to pivot successfully?
4. Who can you talk to for support or accountability around this pivot?

2

2. Change Is Going to Happen—Whether You Are Ready or Not

Let me level with you right from the jump: change does not care if you are ready and it will not ask for permission. It does not check your calendar, your bank account, or your mental health status before it barges in. Change shows up when it wants to—sometimes slow and creeping like fog rolling over the San Bernardino mountains, and sometimes like a damn freight train in the middle of the night. Now, I am not saying that to scare you, I am saying it because it is true. Life has a rhythm to it, and part of that rhythm is movement—constant, unpredictable, sometimes inconvenient movement. Nothing stays the same, not people, not jobs, not relationships, or your health, your routines, or your sense of who you are. The only thing you can count on is that things are going to shift. Sometimes it is a blessing, but sometimes it is a gut punch. But it is always coming and you can either move with it, or get dragged behind it. That is the hard truth a lot of people do not want to hear.

You Cannot Outrun Change

Over the years, I have watched people try to outrun change like it is a suspect they can outmaneuver. They dig in their heels and grip tight to what is familiar. They tell themselves that if they just hang on long enough, the storm will pass and everything will go back to the way it was, but let me tell you something: sometimes the storm is the change and it is not passing, it is here to stay. It is your new normal knocking at the door, and no amount of pretending is going to stop it from coming in.

And I get it—change is uncomfortable as it throws off your routine, makes you question what you thought you knew, makes you feel small, vulnerable, exposed and as human beings - we hate that. We crave familiarity and build our lives around what we know, and once we find something that works—even if it is only kind of working—we tend to stick with it. Here is what I have learned: familiar does not always mean safe and sometimes the very thing we are clinging to is the thing that is keeping us stuck. That job that drains you, that role you no longer fit into, that version of yourself that no longer reflects who you are—it is time to call it what it is: a dead weight.

The Weight of Avoidance

The longer you avoid change, the heavier it gets and you know what I am talking about, you feel it in your shoulders, in your gut, and in the back of your mind. It is that quiet discontent that grows louder over time, that knot in your stomach when you pull into the parking lot at a job you no longer care about or that ache in your chest when you look at your life and wonder, "Is this it?" You tell yourself, "It is not that bad. I can manage" and you push through, numb out, and distract yourself with tasks and to-do lists and streaming services and social media. But no matter the technique you try, the discontent does not leave and it piles up slowly and relentlessly until one day, you wake up and realize you are not living anymore—you are just enduring.

That is the cost of refusing to pivot and the price of holding on too long. Let me be clear: this is not about being ungrateful and it is not about quitting the moment something gets hard. It is about being honest enough to recognize when something has run its course and about respecting yourself enough to say, "This isn't working anymore, and that's okay." The truth is, every season has an expiration date and ignoring that expiration date does not make you strong—it makes you stagnant.

Respect the Whisper Before It Roars

Not all change comes loud and obvious. Sometimes it is subtle and starts as a whisper, a gut feeling or a sense that something is shifting and you cannot always explain it, but you just know. It could be a hobby that starts to feel like a calling, a relationship that no longer energizes you, or even a restlessness you cannot shake. Do not ignore those nudges, as that is life trying to get your attention before it must raise its voice. I have seen what happens when people ignore the whisper. It turns into a shout and if you still do not listen, life will flip the table and leave you picking up the pieces, wondering what just happened. I have lived both ends of that spectrum. I have made quiet pivots where I caught the signs early, and I have also gotten hit upside the head because I did not want to admit it was time to let go. One hurts a lot more than the other.

"The Perfect Time" Is a Myth

Let me save you some time—you are never going to feel 100% ready. There will never be a day when all the lights turn green, your bank account is full, and everyone in your life supports your decision to change. Waiting for perfect timing is just procrastination in disguise and all you have is now and listen to me - now is enough. That does not mean you leap without thinking and it does not mean you act recklessly, but it does mean you start moving. You take inventory and look at your life with clear eyes and ask: "What is working? What is not? What needs to change?" You do not need a full blueprint; you just need to take the next right step. I know that can feel scary and I know it is easier to stay in the loop you already understand, but growth never comes from comfort. It comes from stepping into the unknown with enough faith to believe you will figure it out as you go.

Stagnation Has a Cost

Let me put it in simple terms from grade school science: water that does not move gets stale. It turns green, it starts to stink, and the same thing happens to people. You stop evolving, stop dreaming, stop taking risks—and before long, you are not really living, you are just recycling the same day repeatedly, waiting for something to change on its own. Here is the truth: life does not pivot for you. You must pivot.

This does not mean everything changes overnight, as most pivots happen gradually with a conversation here or a journal entry there. It could be a new idea, a new opportunity, or a moment of clarity you did not expect. These gradual things all add up and lead somewhere—if you are paying attention. Staying where you are because it is familiar, even though it is slowly breaking you, is not strength. Strength is looking the fear in the face and saying, "I'm not going to let you stop me."

Pain Has a Purpose

I would be lying if I told you change was not painful, because sometimes it is very painful and sometimes it means walking away from something you have poured years into. Sometimes it means starting over when you thought you were supposed to be "settled." It can feel like loss, because in many ways, it is loss. Pain has a way of shaping us because it reveals what matters and it tends to scrape off what is fake. It burns away the distractions and forces us to face ourselves honestly – and if you let it, pain will also push you into the next version of your life. I know men who lost their careers, their marriages, their health—and found more purpose in the aftermath than they ever had before and not because they enjoyed the suffering, but because they let it refine them instead of define them. The pivot does not just take you somewhere new—it makes you someone new if you embrace it.

You Do not Have to Be Fearless

You do not have to be fearless to change, you just must be willing - willing to ask the hard questions, willing to make uncomfortable decisions, and willing to let go of what no longer serves you—even if you do not know exactly what is coming next. Fear does not mean you are weak, it means you are human. But courage? Courage is taking the next step while you are afraid. Courage is saying, "I don't have all the answers, but I trust myself enough to figure it out along the way." And here is the thing—you have made it through hard things before and you have pivoted before, even if you did not call it that at the time. Because of that, you have grown, adapted, survived, and evolved. This is just another version of that and you have the tools and you have the grit - you just need to use it.

This chapter is not about bracing for impact and it is not about white-knuckling your way through life, waiting for the next shoe to drop. It is, however, about recognizing that change is not a glitch in the system—it is the system. Change is the design and it is built into the fabric of who we are and how the world works. In every aspect of life, you can see it - the seasons change, the tides change, and you change. This is not something to resist, it is something to respect, so take a deep breath and shake the dust off your feet because the road ahead will not be straight and will not always be smooth - but it will be yours.

Here is what I can promise you: if you keep showing up—honestly, humbly, and willing to grow—you will find strength you did not know you had and you will discover that change is not the end of your story. It is the start of the next chapter, and maybe—just maybe—that chapter will be the one that changes everything.

Reflection & Action

1. What part of this chapter resonated with you most? Why?
2. What is one action you can take this week to apply a principle discussed here?
3. Are there any habits or beliefs you need to let go of to pivot successfully?
4. Who can you talk to for support or accountability around this pivot?

3

3. Knowing When It is Time to Pivot

We do not always see the signs right away. But make no mistake—they are there.

As I said in the prior chapter, sometimes it is a whisper that is subtle and quiet and you start dragging yourself through the day, wondering why even the small things feel heavier than they used to. The job that once made you feel alive? Now it just feels like clocking in and clocking out and the people around you are talking, and you nod and smile, but inside you are somewhere else. You feel disconnected, as if you are just going through the motions and you tell yourself it is just a rough patch—but then that patch starts feeling like the whole damn road.

Other times, the signs come in loud and there is no mistaking it. You dread Mondays—not in the way people joke about it on social media, but in the real, bone-deep kind of way. You wake up and your stomach tightens before your feet even hit the ground. You lie awake at night, your mind chewing on the same questions over and over like a dog with a bone. You find yourself snapping at people who do not deserve it, or withdrawing from the ones who love you. You look around and realize your life somehow turned into something you no longer recognize. Take heart, because that does not always mean something is wrong with you, it might just mean you have outgrown where you are standing.

That is growth and it does not always show up with flashing lights and grand declarations. Most of the time it sneaks in as discomfort, restlessness, or a low hum of dissatisfaction that is easy to dismiss at first. But it keeps humming, and if you do not pay attention to it, that hum turns into a roar. When you start to feel like you are living someone else's life—or living a version of your own life that you no longer want—it is time to listen.

That Feeling You are Trying to Ignore? It is the Starting Line

You know the one I am talking about. That gnawing feeling that creeps in during the in-between moments, like when you are brushing your teeth or driving to work or staring at the ceiling at 2 a.m. when you cannot sleep. It is not always loud, but it is persistent and it asks questions like:
"What are you still doing here?"
"Is this all there is?"
"Do you still want this?"
"Who would you be if you weren't afraid?"

And the more you push it down, the more it pushes back, but listen closely: wanting more does not make you ungrateful. It makes you aware, it means you are still alive inside and that your soul has not gone numb. And yes, that is scary, because it means you might have to do something about it and doing something often feels like blowing everything up, but it does not have to be that dramatic.

You Do not Need to Set Fire to Everything

A pivot is not always about a grand exit and it is not always quitting your job, ending your marriage, moving to a new state, or shaving your head and starting a motorcycle shop in Montana (though, if that is what your gut is telling you, I say go for it).

Sometimes a pivot is internal, quiet, and invisible to everyone else. It can be as simple as this: choosing to say no when you used to say yes, or showing up differently in a space where you have been shrinking, or deciding that your value does not come from your productivity, or accepting that your definition of success has changed—and all of these things are okay. Pivots often start on the inside with a shift in mindset, a moment of clarity, or a new boundary and it is that small choice to stop pretending you are fine when you are not that will make a difference, because even though the world might not even notice at first, you will and that is enough to begin.

The Guilt Trap

One of the biggest barriers to pivoting is not fear—it is guilt. We are trained to be loyal and to stick it out - to be "grateful" for what we have, even when what we have is quietly killing us. We worry we will let someone down—our boss, our family, our friends, or ourselves, and we tell ourselves we should be happy, that other people have it worse or that we are lucky to even have what we have. So we stay in jobs that suck the life out of us, we stay in relationships that do not reflect who we are, or we stay in patterns that used to serve us but now keep us small. Let me offer you something real here: you do not owe anyone your stagnation and you are allowed to change and you are allowed to want more. You are allowed to evolve beyond what people expect of you—and yes, even beyond what you expect of yourself, because gratitude and growth are not mutually exclusive. You can be thankful for what something gave you—and still know it is time to move on.

Taking Inventory

The work starts with honesty and that is where pivots are born. Not in a crisis, not in a breakdown, but in a quiet moment of awareness ask yourself: Am I fulfilled? Do I feel like I am growing or just surviving? Am I showing up as the person I want to be? Is this still me? Be honest with the answers. If the answer is "no" more often than it is "yes," do not ignore that, because that is your signal, your nudge - and you do not need to have a grand plan for it. You do not need to know exactly what is next, but you do need to start paying attention because if you do not take inventory, life eventually will—and usually in a way that is more painful and more disruptive than if you had just listened to yourself in the first place.

When You Stay Too Long

When you stay in a place too long, you start to shrink to fit it and you lose parts of yourself. You get smaller and quiet your dreams or you lower your standards and you settle, and then one day, you look up and you do not recognize the person staring back at you in the mirror. I have seen it happen in the field with guys who stayed in patrol five years longer than they should have or those who climbed the ranks, got the titles, but lost themselves in the process and in that process forgot where they came from and everyone under them paid the price for that.

Why? Because they knew deep down it was time to pivot—but they could not bring themselves to take the first step and they waited too long and when they finally moved, they were exhausted, bitter, and worn out from the delay. Do not let that be you.

The Courage to Question Everything

The first pivot is always the hardest because it calls everything into question - your decisions, your identity, as well as your future. However, once you learn that you can pivot and survive? That you can change course and still be you—sometimes an even better version of you? That is when the fear starts to lose its grip and you realize you are allowed to choose again to redefine who you are or to start over. Remember, you do not have to prove yourself to anyone - you just must be true to yourself. And that, my friend, takes courage.

How You Know it is Time

As I have been talking about this subject, sometimes people ask me, "How do I know for sure it's time to pivot?" The answer? You already know. Maybe not with your head, but your body knows, your gut knows, and that still, small voice inside you? —it knows.

When the work you are doing feels like a costume you are tired of wearing, when your energy is constantly depleted no matter how much sleep you get, when joy feels like something that happened back then, or when you keep imagining another life, and the only reason you are not chasing it is because you are afraid - that is when you know. And again, knowing does not mean you must act impulsively or immediately, it just means you start to explore, to gather information, to ask questions, and imagine possibilities. You open the door to the idea that maybe—just maybe—there is another path.

It Starts with One Step

Remember, you do not have to leap, you just must move tiny step by tiny step and start small with things that are easy to accomplish and check off the list, so update the résumé, have the hard conversation, book the therapy session, take the class, ask the mentor, or write the damn list of dreams you keep stuffing in a drawer. You do not have to figure it all out today, but you do need to start.

Real World Example: Chris Lee – 9-time Emmy Award Winning Film Maker

Chris Lee's life never followed a straight line and if you ask him, he'd probably tell you he would not have wanted it any other way. He is a man who has pivoted more than once—not out of indecision, but out of a quiet courage to follow what felt real at each stage of life. His first chapter began in the United States Marine Corps, where discipline was forged along with a mindset of grit, and an inner stillness under pressure. However, as is the case for many veterans, the transition to civilian life was accompanied by a significant question: what should come next? For a while, Chris drifted and spent his time surfing and playing guitar in Newport Beach, having given himself permission to slow down and breathe.

But even then, something was already stirring, and he started writing— short stories, parts of a novel, thoughts that had nowhere else to go except the page. It wasn't glamorous, but it was real because he wasn't just decompressing; he was discovering something deeper. He wasn't just drawn to the creative life—he was built for it. That led him to college, where he earned a degree in English Literature with an emphasis in Creative Writing. He went all in—reading, writing, editing, surrounding himself with words, but it wasn't the classroom that lit the fire. It was the stories out in the real world and Chris left college early to become a reporter, chasing facts and digging into life with a pen in one hand and purpose in the other. While it was in no way a conventional move, for him it was the right one.

Eventually, he circled back to finish his degree and found himself teaching writing and video production and for nearly a decade, he poured his knowledge and experience into students, helping them find their voices just as he had found his. It was steady work - decent work - but that restless voice inside him started stirring again telling him "You are not done yet." So, he walked away from the safe and predictable and left the pension, the comfort, the security, and the known and proceeded to jump into the unknown—an at-will job with the District Attorney's Office. This spot came with no guarantees and no road map, but that move became a turning point because Chris didn't just find a job—he found his calling.

Today, he serves as a storyteller for the San Bernardino County Sheriff's Employees' Benefit Association (SEBA), giving voice to the people who serve with honor, heart, and quiet heroism. He crafts films and content that capture their journeys, their families, their sacrifices and he does it not just with skill—but with soul and the industry has taken notice. Chris has won nine Emmy Awards for his work (as of this books writing)—recognition not just for polished visuals, but for stories told with depth, clarity, and compassion. Here is the thing about Chris though, if you ask him about those trophies, he won't dwell on the accolades. He will talk about the people in front the lens, the emotional stories of those whose stories he tells, and the mission behind those stories. He will tell you about his family and his pride in his children and their journeys - a testament to a man who has put ego aside and is focusing on service.

That's what makes Chris's pivot so powerful. He didn't chase money, rank, titles or accolades. He chased joy and chose purpose, and in doing so, he stitched together a life that reflects who he is—disciplined but creative, steady but bold, humble but unshakably committed and in doing so the accolades still came. Chris' story reminds us that pivots aren't always linear, that sometimes they come wrapped in uncertainty and will cost us comfort. But when you're willing to leap—when you're willing to trust that the next chapter might just be the one you were made for—you end up not just working but living.

Knowing Chris, I am sure that he is not done pivoting and that's a good thing, because some lives are meant to be written one brave, beautiful chapter at a time. Chris is a perfect example of pivoting and finding new purpose and I am proud to call him my friend.

Final Thoughts: The Power in the Pivot

Let me leave you with this thought: pivoting is not weakness, it is not flakiness, and it most certainly is not quitting. It is an alignment and is about being honest about who you are and where you want to go. It is choosing to evolve on purpose and no, it is not always clean or easy. Sometimes it will feel like tearing down the walls of a house you built with your bare hands, but what if what you are tearing down wasn't a home anymore—but a cage? Pivots set you free to grow, to dream again about what could be, to build something and someone new and never forget, you are worthy of that freedom. Not someday. Not when it is convenient and not when everyone else understands it. The time is now, so stop waiting for permission because you don't need it and if you do, you already have it. The real question is—will you listen?

Flip the page and let's do a worksheet to see just where you are at!

Self-Reflection Worksheet: Is It Time to Pivot?

Take a moment. Get honest. This is not about judgment—it is about clarity.

SECTION 1: Taking Inventory

Instructions: Read each question slowly. Answer with gut honesty. No sugarcoating.

1. What parts of your life feel "off" right now?

(Think work, relationships, health, mindset, faith—whatever comes to mind.)

✎ _____

_____

✎ _____

_____

✎ _____

_____

2. What parts of your life used to bring you joy—but don't anymore?

✎ _____

_____

✎ _____

_____

3. Do you wake up looking forward to the day ahead?

☐ Yes ☐ Sometimes ☐ Rarely ☐ Never

4. What do you find yourself daydreaming about lately?

✎ _____

_____

✎ _____

_____

5. What is something you have been avoiding dealing with? Why?

✎ _____

_____

✎ _____

_____

SECTION 2: Checking Alignment

6. On a scale of 1–10, how aligned do you feel with your values right now?

(1 = not at all, 10 = fully living them)

☐1 ☐2 ☐3 ☐4 ☐5 ☐6 ☐7 ☐8 ☐9 ☐10

7. What value(s) do you feel you are currently compromising, and for what?

✎ _____

_____

✎ _____

_____

8. Are you still proud of the direction your life is headed? Why or why not?

✎ _____

_____

✎ _____

_____

SECTION 3: Inner Voice Check

9. What has your gut been trying to tell you lately?

✎ _____

_____

✎ _____

_____

10. What would you do differently if you were not afraid of failing?

✎ _____

_____

✎ _____

_____

11. What do you *want*—really want—but have not said aloud yet?

✎ _____

_____

✎ _____

_____

SECTION 4: Small, Honest Moves

12. What is one area where you know something needs to shift?

✎ _____

_____

13. What is one small, next step you could take this week to explore that shift?

✎ _____

_____

14. What support do you need? Who can you talk to about this honestly?

✎ _____

_____

Final Word

Write yourself a note. One or two sentences. From your future self—who is already on the other side of the pivot.

✎ *"I know you are scared. But…"*

✎ _____

_____

✎ _____

_____

📓 Reflection & Action

1. What part of this chapter resonated with you most? Why?
2. What is one action you can take this week to apply a principle discussed here?
3. Are there any habits or beliefs you need to let go of to pivot successfully?
4. Who can you talk to for support or accountability around this pivot?

II

Part Two

Re-framing Identity and Purpose

4

4. More Than the Job: Why Your Career Is Not Your Identity

"You are not your rank, your title, or your paycheck. You are the person underneath all that gear."

There is a moment that comes for many of us in uniform—whether you wear a badge, a stethoscope, a suit, or steel-toe boots—when the job becomes more than just work. It becomes who you are and it creeps in slowly. First, it is pride – graduation from an academy or training program. Then it is responsibility – you have learned the job and now people count on you. Then, somewhere along the way, it becomes your identity and if you are not careful, it becomes everything.

I have seen it too many times to count—good people who gave everything to the job and did not know who they were without it. Early in my career, if I am being honest, I did the same thing. If someone said "Who are you," my response was invariably, "I am a cop." But that is not who I was, it was what I did, I had just come to let it define me.......and I did not really like who that guy was. Luckily, I got into woodworking and got back into playing music in bands, and that coupled with marrying a supportive wife (who was a dispatcher and understood the job) allowed me to shift my focus and view of WHO I was back to husband, father, woodworker, musician – not "I am a cop." When I retired from the San Bernardino County Sheriff's Department, I did not have to do a whole lot of soul searching for my next pivot, because I already had my pivot and exit strategy planned out. That does not mean it was easy, because I was not really ready to retire – due to a culmination of injuries to my shoulders (2 replacements), back, knees, and heart, I really was not left with much of a choice and had to tap out.

So, this was not my first pivot - although during the first ones, I did not know what to call them.... life??? In the late 90's, I was working at a municipal police department in the Inland Empire and married with two children in a marriage that was falling apart. When we talked about guilt in the last chapter, trust me, I know. I had moved out of the family home and was staying with a friend and my parents (who are celebrating their 67th year of marriage this year) were putting the screws to me that "you stay together for the kids." I just could not do it. We had tried counseling and the marriage had just become untenable. Neither of us were happy and I would rather have my kids see me single and happy than married and miserable. Not too long later, I met the woman who would become my wife. Jaime was a dispatcher and "got me" .... she understood the job, the pressures, and the stresses - and it was a good thing she did.

It was during this time that I started woodworking, as the friend I was staying with inherited a bunch of woodworking equipment from his grandfather - and a passion was born that would pay dividends for the rest of my life. A few years later, I injured my back on duty, and it spiraled into the type of political nightmare that you usually only read about. There were tremendous politics going on at the department and even though I was injured I was ordered back to work under threat of termination (it could be its own book) and I had enough and decided to make a full-time woodworking business work and I resigned from the police department, bitter and dejected. My wife was still dispatching, so we had insurance, and I started a full-time cabinetry and trim carpentry business and just worked hurt - but I loved what I was doing. My wife may have been scared by the whole thing, but she never doubted me (at least to my face) and always threw her full support behind the pivot.....even helping to install cabinets and work in the shop finishing cabinets. Eventually, I missed law enforcement and felt like I had left something on the table that I was not ready to give up and I went back to the Sheriff's Department, where I worked for the next 16 years - while still running the cabinetry and woodworking business - as well as teaching college at the local junior college. That was again a fortuitous pivot, as right after I was hired, the housing market tanked and the cabinetry field suffered a huge downturn. So, I know what you are going through and facing - you can do this.

So, this chapter is for anyone who has given themselves to a profession and for anyone who has worn the title like a second skin and forgot what it felt like to be anything else. I want to talk to you about what it means to separate your identity from your occupation—and why it is one of the most important pivots you will ever make.

The Job Is What You Do—Not Who You Are

Let us start with something simple that a lot of people struggle to hear: You are not your job. That is not just a feel-good phrase, it is the truth and we live in a culture that teaches us early on to tie our worth to what we do for a living. "What do you want to be when you grow up?" becomes "What do you do for work?" becomes "Who are you?"—and somehow all those questions get answered with the same sentence. If your answer to "Who are you?" is always "I'm a cop" or "I'm a nurse" or "I'm an engineer," then you are building your identity on a foundation that can—and likely will—change.

While it may see rather obvious, jobs end, roles change, and careers evolve or collapse or conclude. If you do not know who you are without the badge, the business, or the office, then when it is gone, you will be gone too. I have watched decorated officers fall apart in retirement and I have seen high-powered professionals crash after layoffs, not because they lost their income—but because they lost their identity. It is like losing your reflection and when you look in the mirror and you do not know who is staring back. That is dangerous, and that is why we need to talk about this.

My Own Reckoning

I spent almost three decades in law enforcement and I was proud of my service and I still am, but I also know how easy it is to get caught up in the culture of constantly proving to yourself and others who you are - even though I consciously tried to avoid it. Every promotion, every commendation, every leadership course—it all felt like affirmation. Like confirmation that I was on the right path and that I was somebody. Looking back now, it is a lot easier to see I was not chasing excellence—I was chasing identity and even though I focused on not becoming the job, it still crept in at times and then the job ended. Retirement sounds like a celebration and for some, it is. But for me, it was like hitting a wall, partly because I did not go out totally on my terms....it was due to a career of trauma and injuries that went untreated and I went from constant radio chatter and high-stakes decisions to dead silence. Nobody was calling, nobody was asking for direction, and nobody needed Sergeant

Snow, and truth be told, while I did not miss the job and the B.S., I did miss the camaraderie and "the team." Remember this.... the badge, uniform, title, position, etc..... are all things you DO.... they are NOT WHO YOU ARE.

The Dangers of Over-Identification

When your career becomes your identity, you risk three things:

1. Burnout - If your whole sense of self-worth is tied to your job, then every mistake you make becomes a threat to your value and every bad day is not just a bad day—it reflects who you are. That is a fast track to exhaustion.
2. Isolation - If you allow your work to become your identity, every-thing else becomes secondary—family, friends, hobbies, and your health and eventually, the people who love you start feeling like strangers, and when the job ends, you will quickly come to realize you are alone.
3. Crisis in Transition - Whether by choice or by force, your career will shift and if you have wrapped your whole identity in it, that shift will feel like death. People fall into depression, addiction, or desperation—not because they lost a job, but because they lost themselves.

Signs You've Let the Job Take Over

So, how do you know if you have let your career become who you are as sometimes, we do not even realize it is happening. Here are a few red flags to watch for: You only talk about work in social settings or you struggle to answer the question, "What do you do for fun?" You do not take vacations—or when you do, you feel guilty. Your self-worth rises and falls with performance reviews, you are uncomfortable being around people outside your field, or you have no vision for your life beyond retirement or promotion.

If even one of these hits close to home, do not panic. You are not alone, but it may be time to start pulling your identity back from the job.

Building an Identity Beyond the Job

So how do you reclaim yourself when your career has become your identity? You do not have to quit your job or throw away everything you have built; you just must start expanding your self-concept and here are a few ideas of how to do that.

1. Reconnect With Your Core Values - Who are you when nobody's watching? What do you believe in? What kind of person do you want to be? Strip away the uniform and titles, and start writing those answers down. For me, it came down to service, leadership, integrity, and legacy because those values did not belong to the badge, they belonged to me. The job just gave me one way to live them out.

2. Reinvest in Your Roles Outside of Work - REMEMBER - You are more than a cop, a fireman, a nurse, a CEO, or whatever job you have, you are a father, a spouse, a friend, a mentor, a neighbor. It is time to start showing up in those roles with the same energy you bring to work, because I will be honest — I neglected some of those roles for years. The job always came first and I was always there to pick up the phone and roll out for the job, but reconnecting with my family and my community gave me purpose that did not require a paycheck.

3. Develop Interests and Hobbies That Do Not Involve Work - This is something that I always told my people who worked with and for me, as well as the students I taught in the academy or academic classes.

You MUST have passions and hobbies that are outside of your job. Start woodworking. Volunteer. Learn photography. Travel. Coach. Build. Paint. Join a band. Whatever it is, make space for something that brings you joy and is not tied to your job because it will allow you an outlet to leave work at work and just breathe......and this should start as early in your career as possible. As noted in the last chapter, woodworking became my therapy about 7 years into my career and was a life saver. It was quiet and honest with hands in the dust and a mind at peace (except when I was trying to figure out how to fix a screw up). No uniform was required, just craft and care.

I would also tie keeping the friends you have into this. All too often, especially in the first responder realm, we start to only hang out with those we work with because "they are the only ones who "get" me" ...... this is dangerous and very akin to having an echo chamber. Keeping the friends you had before the job helps keep you grounded and helps you remember who you are. I still have the same best friend from 5th grade - he is a math whiz and does accounting - and we can go months without talking and fall right back into where we were when we last talked. These are the friends to keep - they do not buy into your "persona" because they know you and will call you out on the bullshit. Love you Greg.

4. Mentor Without Tying Your Worth to It - You do not have to lead a department to lead people, share your wisdom, or encourage younger folks in your field. The important caveat to that I would share is that you do it as a person, not as a rank. Mentorship helped me stay connected without feeling like I had to stay "in charge" and it reminded me that leadership is not about control—it is about investment.

What the Job Can Be

This is not about turning your back on your profession, in fact that could not be farther from the truth. I believe in giving 100% to the work you do (remember, hard work wins), and I believe in honoring the oath, serving with heart, and striving for excellence, but you can do all that without losing yourself in it. Think of your career like a vehicle. It can take you places and it can be a source of meaning, but it is not the destination—it is the ride. You do not become the car just because you are driving it. Let the job be something you do well—not something you have to be.

When the Pivot Comes

Eventually, the pivot will come and maybe you will leave the job or the job will leave you - hell, the whole industry could change and when that day arrives, you do not want to be caught scrambling for identity. You want to have one already built—firm, clear, rooted. You want to be the kind of person who can say: "The work I did mattered, but that was not the whole story, because I mattered, even without it."

And this is another area that I want you to think about and remember, because in a lot of jobs you will hear, "We are a family" or "Family comes first." Those are cute slogans and sayings, but very few times have I worked for people who A. believed it truly or B. lived it. At the end of the day, you are a position number - even in the smallest of organizations - they will do their best to convince you that the organization cannot go on without you, and you may even try and convince yourself of this as I did: "Well there is no one with my qualifications to take over the MAIT Division and run it with the care I do." Then you go out on an injury and do not hear from anyone for a year while you are trying to rehab - other than to maybe inventory some equipment and you think to yourself: I thought we were a family? Then you do get a call to come pick up your gear from your office because they filled your position because they just could not leave it vacant. As soon as you are gone, your position will be filled - remember that - you are not irreplaceable, and it is that way from the lowest rung of the ladder to the boss himself.

Real Talk: Questions to Ask Yourself

So, let's do a little self-reflection and see where we are at. Let's take a minute and grab a notebook, go for a walk, or just sit in silence. Ask yourself the following questions and jot down the first thought to come to mind without editorializing yourself: Who am I beyond my job? What relationships have I neglected in pursuit of career success? If I could not work tomorrow, what would give my life meaning? What gifts do I have that are not tied to my title? What kind of legacy do I want to leave behind? These are not easy questions. But they are worth asking now—before you hit the pivot.

Real World Example: Paul Pantani – The Transition Drill Podcast

Let me tell you about Paul Pantani. He's not famous (yet), and he is not someone you've seen giving a TED Talk or plastered across social media as a "thought leader," but he is the kind of man I've come to admire—the kind that has lived, pivoted, led, stumbled, pivoted again, and kept going with grit, self-reflection, and a deep sense of purpose. Paul's story doesn't start with a grand plan or a childhood dream playing out exactly how he imagined. It starts like a lot of ours do— complicated. During his teenage years, Paul often disagreed with his father's authority, which he perceived as strict at the time. Nonetheless, certain experiences from that period had a lasting influence and became more significant in later years. One of those was his father's decision to enroll him in Catholic high school, which at the time, Paul probably saw as another form of control, but years later, he came to see it as a gift—a better education, a better environment, and maybe even the first nudge toward something higher than just getting by.

But teenage Paul wasn't ready for that growth just yet and he resisted. When his father forbade him from playing football because of a mild knee injury and a cautious doctor's warning, Paul refused to return to baseball—his father's sport—and instead, walked away from athletics altogether. Academics took a hit too and he coasted with D's, hung around a crowd that drank and smoked, and rolled into his senior year with a 1.97 GPA. As he'd later say with a wry smile, "I showed him." Then came one of those turning points, when his guidance counselor pulled him aside and gave it to him straight—if he didn't turn things around, his future would be, at best, limited. Something about that stuck and while maybe the idea of becoming a police officer had already taken root, Paul couldn't really trace it to any specific moment or influence. There were no police officers in his family, no deep mentorship from a neighborhood officer - maybe it was just something buried in the subconscious—his father saying that police officers deserved respect. Whatever it was, it pointed him toward a path.

After graduation, Paul thought about the military as a way to bridge the years until he could be hired as a cop, but he allowed others to influence his decision and they talked him out of it, saying one enlistment wouldn't be worth much unless he planned to make a career of it— something he still considers one of his biggest regrets. Instead, at 19, Paul landed in a spot as a Police Cadet., which opened the door to what would become a nearly 20-year run in the same department. Here's where the story takes a sharper turn. Paul didn't plan on college, but the job required an associate's degree, so he got one. Then the mother of his children—who held a bachelor's—became a silent motivator to earn his own, not for himself but to show their kids that education mattered. Then came a master's degree in Economic Crime Management, because at that point, he was a fraud detective, and it made sense to double down on that specialty. One pivot led to another and before long, Paul was teaching college students—undergraduates and graduates alike, how to investigate, how to think, how to approach complex financial crimes with integrity and clarity.

He served nearly 35 years in law enforcement and retired as a Commander in December 2023. But retirement didn't mean stepping back, it meant stepping into something new—even if he wasn't sure what that would be. In 2021, he launched the Transition Drill podcast, sitting down with veterans and first responders to talk about what it really means to leave a mission-driven life behind and build something new. The idea was born from his own questions—how do you transition out of law enforcement or a life of service with purpose? How do you carry the weight of all those years and still walk forward?

Paul thought the transition would be easier and figured with his leadership experience, degrees, and track record, landing a second career would be a smooth process, but it wasn't. The roles that came along weren't the right fit with either long commutes, relocations, or expectations that didn't align with his values or lifestyle. So, he pivoted again and leaned into the podcast, building a platform for honest conversations and community. It's still growing, still gaining traction, and still evolving.

And Paul? He's still in the pivot. He is still searching and moving forward with his eyes open and his head up, and that is what I want people to understand—pivoting isn't a one-time thing. It's not always clean or linear, sometimes it's full of questions that don't get answered right away. But Paul's story is proof that growth doesn't end with retirement and purpose doesn't expire when the badge comes off. You can build something new, you can reinvent yourself and you can keep becoming whatever it is you see—if you're willing to work, reflect, and stay connected to the mission beneath the surface. Paul did. And he's not done yet.

A Final Word

While we talk about you not becoming your job, never forget, there is a lot of honor in showing up for your work, in giving your best, and in leaving things better than you found them, but do not confuse your duty with your identity. The badge, the briefcase, the title—they are the tools, the chapters, and the seasons of your journey and life, but they are not you. You are the person who carried the weight with dignity. You are the soul who showed up even when it hurt. You are the voice your kids remember. You are the friend who stood tall, and you are the mentor someone looks up to. This is an important fact to remember - when all the job titles fade, when the nameplate comes off the desk and the locker is empty— You are still here. You are strong, whole, and still worthy. Please do not wait until the end of your career to figure that out.

Start now.

📕 Reflection & Action

1. What part of this chapter resonated with you most? Why?
2. What is one action you can take this week to apply a principle discussed here?
3. Are there any habits or beliefs you need to let go of to pivot successfully?
4. Who can you talk to for support or accountability around this pivot?

5

5. The Second Mission: Finding Purpose After Retirement or in the Pivot

"You were made for more than one mission. If you are still breathing, you are still needed."

This is a companion chapter to the last one and offers a little more insight into purpose with some real stories of real people, my friends, who have not only lived through pivots but thrived.

Retirement. Pivot. Transition.

Whatever you call it, there comes a day when your first chapter ends— and a new one begins. As we have discussed, it can come as a whisper or as a storm, but it comes. As I have discussed, I remember the day I hung up my badge for good and after almost three decades in law enforcement, I walked out of the station for the last time. There was a ceremony, some handshakes, a few kind words, and then, silence. No radio, no calls, no uniform, no schedule, and no more roll call or going in service, just me and the quiet. At first and most of the time, it is a wonderful feeling but then at times, that silence can be deafening

- even in a shop full of tools running. For some, it is freedom, while for others, it is disorientation and for many of us who gave our lives to a profession, especially one rooted in service, the hardest part is not stopping the work but figuring out what matters now. This chapter is about that next mission and about finding a new purpose when the old one is complete. It is for anyone who is retired, changing careers, or just starting to realize that their "what now?" does not have a map.

The Myth of the Finish Line (Retirement)

This section is a note to those on the cusp of or thinking about retirement. Let me start with a truth I wish more people would tell each other: Retirement is not the finish line, but merely a shift in assignment. We spend so much of our lives working toward retirement that it starts to feel like the goal and once we cross that line, life gets easy. Beaches, grand kids, golf or maybe a cabin in the woods and long morning walks with black coffee. For a while, that is great because you have earned it, and rest is important. Eventually though, if you are wired like most high-purpose people, the quiet stops being peaceful and starts being...unsettling, because it turns out, we were not just built for relaxation. We were built for purpose. Maybe not the same kind of hustle as before—but something meaningful that puts your hands to use and your heart back in motion. Something that makes you feel like you still matter.

Because you do.

Why Purpose Matters (Especially After the Pivot)

Let us talk about why this matters so much, especially for those coming out of high-commitment careers. When you have lived with purpose for decades, whether in uniform, in a clinic, a classroom, or a boardroom, you get used to being part of something bigger than yourself. There's a structure, a mission, a responsibility, and an identity. Then, suddenly, that is gone and without purpose, people drift and can become depressed, isolated and sometimes even physically sick. Multiple studies indicate that retirees who possess a strong sense of purpose tend to have increased longevity, encounter fewer chronic health conditions, and report higher levels of overall well-being compared to those lacking such purpose. I am sure that everyone who is reading this knows of people who have passed away shortly after retiring if they just sat at home watching TV and not doing anything productive, while those who found a second purpose often live into their 90's and beyond. Why is this? It is because the human spirit is designed for contribution. We do not age out of meaning and we may change how we serve—but not why.

Three Questions That Lead You to Your Next Purpose

So, let's find our next purpose because it is when the job ends that the real work begins—the work of rediscovery. There is no universal blueprint for this, but in talking to people who have lived it, I have found three questions that can help start the journey.

1. What do I still care about? Strip away the paycheck, the title, the schedule - what are the things that still pull at your heart? Is it kids? Justice? Healing? Craft? Nature? Faith? Mentorship? This is an important question because purpose does not start with "What can I do?" It starts with "What do I care about?" For me, part of that answer came slowly because I had a successful woodworking business already going on and I was able to help people achieve their vision of their homes and what they could be - especially restorations. But I still wanted to do

more to serve, and that realization led me to mentorship, writing, and speaking. I am using different tools—but I still have the same mission: serve with strength, clarity, and heart.

2. What have I learned that others need? You have lived, you have failed, you have overcome, and you have wisdom that textbooks cannot teach and somewhere, someone needs it. Maybe it is younger people in your field, kids in your community, or a local nonprofit or a struggling friend or your own family. Purpose lives in passing it on and let me tell you— there's power in giving back without needing the credit because that is the kind of legacy that does not wear a badge or need a paycheck. That is character-level impact.

3. What do I want to be remembered for? This is one of the existential questions of life.... Not what title or awards, but who you were and how you showed up. What is your legacy going to be? This question is not about ego, it is about vision and if you want to be remembered as someone who lifted others, gave generously, stayed humble, or never stopped growing, then start living like that now. Your next purpose should align with that vision and every day you spend aligning with your core values is a day well lived.

Legacy

Since number three above, speaks a bit about legacy, I want to delve in a little deeper here because I think people misunderstand what legacy truly is. Legacy is not the plaque on the wall they give you when you leave an assignment or your name stitched on a jacket with a fancy title next to it. Legacy is whether things still run the right way when you are not there to run them - it is the habits that outlive you, the standards that don't bend because you're not in the room, and the people who make better calls because you trained them to.

When I worked at Victor Valley College, my partner and boss Rand had a favorite saying: "Leave it better than you found it" and that applied to people, as well as the organization. That wasn't about heroics, it was about custody—of a scene, a team, a family, or a life. Legacy is custody taken seriously, day after day.

You may be asking, "Why does legacy matter?" I will tell you why - when you know what you want to leave behind, your decisions sharpen up, you stop drifting, you feel the weight of tomorrow in the choice you make today, you cut corners less, you invest more, and you quit chasing applause, because applause dies fast. Impact doesn't. If you've ever walked into a unit and felt the culture before anyone spoke—that's legacy. Someone codified standards, someone told the story behind the rules, someone kept showing up the same way, for a long time, and you can feel their fingerprints long after they've rotated out.

So what is legacy if not titles and accolades? Well, if it collapses when you step away, it wasn't legacy, it was ego with good PR and we have all worked for those people in an organization. True legacy is character under pressure, competence shared and not hoarded. It is consistency— the same rules for everyone, even when it costs you. It's courage to tell the truth and own the miss. And it's contribution—time, tools, and training invested where you don't personally benefit, but you do so for the betterment of other people. The world will put your titles on a shelf, but who cares if you cannot look at yourself in the mirror at the end of the day. It is your people who will live with your systems and your standards and promote those ideal, so build for your people.

The 5 C's (keep this in your field notebook) are things to think about when we discuss legacy and they are:

1. **Character** — Who you are when it's inconvenient, because integrity is expensive on the right day. Own your shit - if you screw up, take the hit.
2. **Competence** — Do the job well, and teach the why, not just the how. Skill without transfer dies with you and we have all seen the people who get a bit of specialized knowledge and then want to hoard it all so that everyone has to come to them for the answers - do not be that guy. Give away your knowledge and skills and they will come back to you.
3. **Consistency** — Small, repeatable actions: be on time, squared away, no special deals.
4. **Courage** — Make the hard calls and talk straight. As mentioned in character, admit the mistake and fix the system.
5. **Contribution** — This may be the most important of the five: pour all your knowledge into others until they don't need you and then comes the most important part of it - you cheer them on when they pass you.

To build legacy, you need to do a few things:

1. Codify your standards: write five non-negotiables you want attached to your name and make them short, clear, and enforceable and then post them where you work. If it isn't written, it isn't real.
2. Replace yourself on purpose: This is also a great leadership strategy, because we should be training up our replacements. Name two or three people who could carry your role, but do not just hand them steps; hand them your decision tree—what you look at first, what you weigh, and what you never compromise on, while also giving them some leeway to improvise and explore.

3. System > hero status: Turn your good habits into SOPs, checklists, templates, and drills. While I love a hero story as much as anyone, it is concrete systems that hold the line when nobody's watching - and you (or anyone for that matter) cannot always be there when the proverbial poop hits the fan.

4. Tell the story behind the rule: This is one that I always struggled with in poor leaders because they just wanted you to follow the rule because "they said so." That is a horrible strategy. People obey orders; they carry stories, so if there's a policy because someone got hurt, say that. Do not be afraid to tell people the "why" and if you tie the guideline to a human being and a story, you usually have a lesson learned.

5. Guard your name: Assume every text, post, and comment lives forever and act like your granddaughter will read it - because she might. In this age of the internet and social media, things live forever. People lose jobs or get cancelled because of things they said years ago, or a halloween costume they wore a decade ago - do not risk it. Think about about what you say before you say it and ESPECIALLY before you post it on the ole interwebs!

6. Serve beyond your lane: Mentor someone who can't pay you back, volunteer where nobody knows your résumé, and share your knowledge broadly with no expectation of recognition. This is another important thing to remember because it help to keep keeps your motives clean and your skills sharp and it fills that need for service and purpose that we all have.

Some of the pitfalls of trying to build legacy can be: Chasing credit, because if you need your name on it to care, it is not legacy, it is ego. Do not confuse being busy with being effective - just because you have a full calendar does not mean you are living a life of impact. As we have talked about, do not wait for someday - legacy is built in calendar blocks, not in retirement speeches. It is built on a lifetime of hard work and integrity. The final pitfall that can be intoxicating to many - especially those with ego is making yourself indispensable. This may seem like a great thing to many because, "Hey, I am making myself better for the team," but the reality of it is that if only you can do it, you've built a trap, not a team.

I have seen really sharp employees flame out because everything depended on them. They ran hot, fixed everything, and left nothing that could be repeated, and the day they walked, quality walked with them. That is not the standard we want to achieve - no, the standard is you hand off a binder so clear your successor can carry the mission out on a bad day with low sleep and still get it right.

Build your legacy like a good joint in the shop—clean, hidden, and strong enough to outlast the maker. You don't need applause for that, you just need intention, repetition, and a willingness to train others until they don't need you. When your name comes off the roster and the work still runs honest, tight, and fair—that's legacy. That's the good kind of invisible.

What Purpose Can Look Like in the Second Half

You do not have to start a nonprofit, win an Emmy, beat a disease, or build a movement to have purpose, as purpose is not about scale, but about alignment. I want to share with you a few ways people rediscover meaning after retirement or a major life pivot:

Mentorship: Guiding the next generation in your field.
    Artisan Work: Turning craft into expression (woodworking, painting,

writing, etc.).

Service: Volunteering with veterans, youth, or faith groups.

Teaching: Offering workshops, classes, or storytelling events.

Family: Investing deeply in your role as a parent, grandparent, or caregiver.

Counseling: Becoming a coach or support figure for others navigating change.

Faith or Spiritual Leadership: Stepping into a deeper walk and helping others do the same.

Travel With Purpose: Not just sightseeing—but meaningful connections, service abroad, or pilgrimage.

You do not have to do everything, just do something that matters to you.

The Lie of "I'm Too Old" or "It's Too Late"

Let me address a lie that creeps in for a lot of people during this season: "It's too late for me" or "I am too old." That is nonsense. Do a little research and you will find that Colonel Sanders did not start KFC until his 60s and Laura Ingalls Wilder did not publish her first book until her 60s. I know retired police officers who became counselors, musicians, and carpenters after 50. I am 57 as of the writing of this book, and I have never felt more on purpose than I do right now. You are not too late, you are just different now—maybe wiser, slower, more deliberate, but that is not a liability, it is a gift. Use it.

A Toolbox for the Transition

So, let me give you a few tools I have learned from others—and used myself at times—when the question of purpose gets cloudy.

1. Daily Stillness - You need quiet time to hear your deeper self. Turn off your phone, go somewhere quiet with no distractions, just stillness. Five minutes a day is enough to begin. Sit with yourself in silence and ask, "What am I being drawn to?"

2. Reverse Journaling - The act of having to think and put your thoughts on paper can help figure out what you want to do. Instead of asking yourself "What did I do today?" try asking "What gave me energy today?" and "What drained me?"

3. Values Clarification Exercises - Identifying your core values will anchor your next chapter. To do this, use lists of values (e.g., from Brené Brown or Barrett Values Centre), then narrow it down to your top 5.

4. Life Timeline Mapping - Map out your life and things you have done will help you to recognize patterns, peak moments, and key pivots by drawing a timeline of your life, marking highs, lows, career moves, family changes, etc. and reflect on what gave you purpose in each season.

5. Purpose Statements - Write yourself a guiding sentence can keep you focused when life feels uncertain, i.e.: "I exist to [action] for [people/group] so that [desired impact]."

6. Mentorship & Networking - This is a good way to gain insight as others often see your potential more clearly than you do, so reach out to former colleagues, church leaders, or community mentors and ask them what they see in you or what they'd call on you for.

7. Volunteerism & Service Projects - Doing this can give you real-life trial runs of new passions, i.e.: Habitat for Humanity, Community youth coaching, Veteran support organizations, or Local arts, education, or environmental causes

8. Coaching or Counseling - As with mentorship, a trained outsider can help you process and redirect with clarity. This would include Life coaches (purpose, transition, or career focus), faith-based

counselors, or therapists specializing in life transitions or retirement.

9. Continuing Education / Classes - If you aren't sure, find something that sparks a little interest as learning ignites curiosity and may uncover latent purpose. Check with your local Community college or online with "Master Class," or even local workshops through your town or city.

Final Thoughts

Remember this, it's okay not to know yet what you want to do, as purpose often comes after the pivot, not before. Don't just chase a passion, follow your curiosity as it's quieter but more sustainable and remember that purpose evolves. What you are here for today may not be what you are here for tomorrow and in this, we can help clarify what aligns with your purpose.

📘 Reflection & Action

1. What part of this chapter resonated with you most? Why?
2. What is one action you can take this week to apply a principle discussed here?
3. Are there any habits or beliefs you need to let go of to pivot successfully?
4. Who can you talk to for support or accountability around this pivot?

6

6. Ego: The Hidden Barrier to Growth

"The ego whispers, 'Do not change. You are fine.' Growth says, 'You can be more.' You get to choose which voice you follow."

Every person who has worn a badge, commanded a room, led a team, or succeeded in any profession knows the quiet temptation of ego. It is not always loud or arrogant, sometimes it looks like confidence while other times, it masquerades as pride in a job well done. Word to the wise however - if you are not careful, ego does not just influence your decisions—it takes over and starts driving the whole car. I have felt it, I have fed it, and I have been humbled by it. Ego is one of the biggest obstacles to a successful pivot because ego hates uncertainty and it hates being a beginner again. Ego wants control, recognition, praise, and identity. The crux of the issue though is this: if you want to pivot— whether that is retiring, changing careers, improving a relationship, or evolving who you are—you are going to have to confront your ego.

This chapter is about that confrontation. It is about understanding what ego is, how it shows up in our lives, how it holds us back, and what it takes to grow beyond it.

What Ego Really Is

Let us start by defining ego—not in some philosophical or psychological way, but in the way I have seen it play out in real life. Ego is the voice that says, "I am what I do. I am what I have. I am what people think of me." Ego thrives on identity, appearance, status, and control and one of its most dangerous aspects is that it clings to being right. It fears vulnerability and believes that success is proof of worth, and failure is personal shame. Ego says: "I've been doing this for 20 years—I know better." "They can't talk to me like that." "If I step down, I'll look weak." "I can't admit I need help." "I am not starting over. That is beneath me."

While some of those thoughts might feel justified, they often come from fear - a fear of being less, a fear of being ordinary, a fear of looking bad in front of others, or a fear of losing control. Ego is not confidence; it is insecurity dressed up in armor of self-righteousness and that armor will keep you from growing.

How Ego Shows Up (Especially for High-Achievers)

For people who have had long careers in leadership or service—especially in law enforcement, the military, medicine, or business—ego can sneak in unnoticed because after all, we are trained to be confident, to take charge and to lead. While that is not completely wrong, the line between strength and ego is thin and when you cross it, here's how ego tends to show up:

1. Resisting Change - Ego hates change because it threatens control and if you have built your identity around being the boss, the expert, the go-to person—what happens when you leave the job?

Your ego will resist that pivot as hard as it possibly can because it feels like death.

2. Over-identifying with Your Role - "I'm a sergeant." "I'm the CEO." "I'm the provider." All fine in a way, until you no longer are, because your ego will convince you that you are whatever that role is, and when that role ends, it leaves you feeling worthless or lost.

3. Taking Things Personally - Ah, my personal kryptonite at home that I still fight with.... Feedback? An attack. Criticism? Disrespect. A changed plan? A betrayal. Your ego reacts emotionally because it is fragile and it turns everything into a referendum on your worth and instead of communicating through it, we become defensive and react emotionally.

4. Competing Instead of Connecting - Ego sees everyone else as competition and says, "They're younger, better, faster," and either puts them down or tries to outdo them, a mindset that isolates you.

5. Avoiding Help - Ego tells you that asking for help is weakness, that therapy is for other people, that retirement groups are lame, or that admitting confusion means failure. All of that is nonsense— but ego will fight tooth and nail to protect its image.

What Happens When Ego Runs the Show

So, where does that road take us? If you let ego lead your life, here is what eventually happens:

1. You Stop Learning - Your ego says, "I already know," where growth says, "I'm always learning." When you stop being teachable, you stop growing.

2. You Burn Out - Your ego must constantly prove itself to everyone and that leads to overwork, stress, and exhaustion and when you

inevitably fail or slow down, ego has no capacity for grace.

3. You Push People Away - Your ego protects itself by building walls and it will not let people in, will not admit weakness, and will not say "I'm sorry." That destroys relationships—especially when you are transitioning or struggling.

4. You Miss the Pivot - The longer you listen to ego, the harder it is to recognize when it is time to change and when the pivot finally comes, you are unprepared and bitter—because ego did not allow you to soften into the new season.

How to Quiet the Ego and Grow

Ego will always be there and there really is nothing wrong with ego in the right amounts, but it does not have to be in charge. Here is how I have learned—and am still learning—to quiet it.

1. Practice Humility, Not Humiliation - Humility is not thinking less of yourself, it is thinking of yourself less often. It is admitting, "I do not know everything. I am still learning." You can do this by small things and acts: ask for feedback, say "I was wrong," or acknowledge when someone else has a better idea. Every time you do, ego loses a little power—and you gain more peace.

2. Let Go of the Need to Impress - In the age of social media, where everyone wants to share their highlight reel, remember that not everything you do has to be posted, praised, or perfect. There is a quiet kind of strength in doing something well and telling no one - paint a picture, build a cabinet, mentor a kid, pray, serve, and do it because it matters—not because it is seen.

3. Surround Yourself with Grounded People - Find others who are not impressed by your résumé, someone who sees you, the person, not the position. We all need someone who will call us out when ego

takes over and those relationships will not only keep you honest, they will hold you when everything else gets shaken.

4. Reconnect With Service - The fastest way to shrink ego is to serve someone who can do nothing for you in return, so volunteer, teach, encourage, and listen because ego cannot coexist with selfless service. Try it and watch how small your pride gets when you wash someone else's feet—literally or metaphorically.

5. Embrace Beginner Energy - Here is one ego will fight you on.... there's power in starting over, so take a class, try a new hobby, or walk into a room where you are the least experienced person there. Yes, your ego will protest, but your spirit will thank you because it is hungry to grow in positive ways and that hunger is sacred.

Real World Example #5: Russell Groenheim - School Counselor

When I think of someone who embodies putting ego aside and being humble, the first one I think of is my brother in law, Russ. I've known Russ over 45 years, though our relationship has evolved in ways I never could have predicted. Long before he became my brother-in-law, Russell was my junior high church leader—the guy who showed up every week to invest in kids who were still figuring out who they were. At that age, you don't always appreciate what that kind of dedication means, but looking back now, I see it clearly. He wasn't just there to lead youth group activities or teach Bible lessons, he was there to show us what consistency, humility, and faith in action look like.

Russell had this way of meeting you exactly where you were—never talking down to you, but never letting you off the hook either. He knew how to listen, and he had a knack for asking the kind of questions that made you think long after the conversation ended. Whether we were on a youth trip, sitting around after a service, or just hanging out at the church, he carried himself with a calmness that made you feel like you could trust him with the stuff you didn't tell anyone else. For me, as a teenager trying to make sense of my own path, he was one of those rare adults who genuinely made an impact.

That kind of heart for people didn't stop with youth ministry. Today, Russell is a school counselor in the Fontana Unified School District, and he continues to do the same kind of work—just in a different setting. Every day, he works with kids who are facing challenges that go far beyond academics. These are students navigating anxiety, family struggles, peer pressure, and the weight of growing up in a world that moves faster than they can keep up. And just like he did in church years ago, Russell meets them where they are. He leads social-emotional learning programs, helps kids build confidence, and creates a safe place for them to talk about the hard stuff.

Now that Russell is family, I've had the chance to see another side of him—the husband, the father, the brother-in-law who still carries that same quiet strength. I've watched him step into situations that would overwhelm most people and handle them with patience and grace and it is the same character I saw in him all those years ago, just deeper now, built through experience and the kind of faith that doesn't waver when life gets messy. Russell has gone on ride a longs with me and when we would get lunch with my partners, he would always thank them for doing the job they were doing and putting others needs before their own. That is humility and gratitude.

Russell's story reminds me that some pivots aren't dramatic—they're steady and deliberate. He could have chosen a different career path, one that didn't demand so much emotional energy, but he chose to invest in people. That's not an easy choice, because it means being present when kids are hurting, being the one who listens when no one else will, and carrying the weight of knowing you can't fix everything, but you can at least show up and showing up is often the pivot that changes someone's life.

When I think about The Pivot and what it means to adjust course in life, Russell's journey is a perfect example, because he didn't pivot away from who he was—he pivoted deeper into his calling. From youth ministry to school counseling, he's continued to serve, to mentor, and to remind people—young and old—that they matter. He's proof that your greatest impact often comes from choosing consistency over recognition and people over comfort.

For me, having Russell as both a mentor in my youth and now as a brother-in-law is something I don't take lightly. He's part of the reason I understand the value of mentorship, the importance of investing in the next generation, and the power of choosing service over self. His life is a living reminder that sometimes the greatest pivots are made quietly, through years of faithfulness, until one day you look back and realize just how many lives have been changed because someone like Russell decided to show up and keep showing up.

Final Thoughts

"If you think someone ruined your life, you're right—it's you." That line, often pinned on Nietzsche, hits like a punch to the gut because it doesn't leave you much room to hide. It strips away the excuses, the finger-pointing, and the "what-ifs," leaving you with the hard truth: the only person who can wreck your life is the one staring back at you in the mirror and usually the one doing the wrecking is EGO.

Life is going to throw curveballs—unfair ones, blindsiding ones and people will let you down, and circumstances will cut you off at the knees but Nietzsche's point wasn't that these things don't matter. It is that your response to them matters more, because you can't control the storm, but you can decide whether you're going to stand there and get soaked, or start building a damn shelter.

Personal responsibility is the heart of it and the day you stop letting ego blame others and stop waiting for someone else to fix things and start taking ownership of your life is the day you start to move forward. Your story isn't written by your boss, your ex, or whatever obstacle just rolled into your path, it is written by how you choose to react and the steps you take next.

Nietzsche believed in the strength of the individual to rise above their own limitations. That's the pivot—looking at the challenge in front of you and deciding it's not the end of the road but the start of a new one. You take your scars, your setbacks, and your mistakes, and you turn them into fuel.

Ego wants you to blame others and blaming others for the mess you're in feels good in the short term—it's like a sugar rush but it keeps you stuck, and the longer you hold on to that, the less power you have to change anything. Nietzsche's challenge is simple but brutal: stop pointing fingers. You want something different? Then do something different. When you own your part in the story, the whole game changes. You stop being a victim and start being the author, and while that doesn't mean life will suddenly be easy, it does mean you will have the grit to push through and create something better because you know the power sits in your hands.

At its core, that quote is a wake-up call because it is telling you that no matter how rough the road has been, you still have the pen. You still get to choose the next chapter.

Letting go of ego isn't about weakness, it's about strength—the kind of quiet, grounded strength that allows you to stand in the middle of uncertainty and say, "I don't have all the answers, but I'm willing to learn." Ego will tell you to fake it, to preserve appearances, to protect your pride, but the pivot—real, lasting transformation—demands something deeper: humility, courage, and honesty. I've stood at enough crossroads to know this much: when you are pivoting, your ego will kick and scream and it will tell you you're too far along to start over, too old to try something new, and too important to take a risk that might bruise your image but ego is loud and hollow and it is not your true north, your soul is.

The core truth of this is that every meaningful change in life requires the death of some ego and that voice in your head that's obsessed with being right, being admired, being safe—it's the same voice that will talk you out of growth if you let it. When you set it down, even just for a moment, you create space for something better: clarity, peace, and purpose. Letting go of ego doesn't mean you lose your edge, it means you sharpen it in a different way—less concerned with proving yourself, more focused on being yourself and the more you do that, the more resilient, connected, and authentic your pivot will be. You don't need ego to pivot, you need truth, grit, grace, and maybe most of all, you need the guts to walk away from who you were pretending to be so you can become who you actually are.

Let go. Pivot forward.

Reflection & Action

1. What part of this chapter resonated with you most? Why?
2. What is one action you can take this week to apply a principle discussed here?
3. Are there any habits or beliefs you need to let go of to pivot successfully?
4. Who can you talk to for support or accountability around this pivot?

7

7. You Cannot Move Forward If You Will Not Let Go

One of the main things about change that no one really likes to talk about is that sometimes the hardest part is not the uncertainty ahead— it is the grip we have on what we should have let go of a long time ago. Most times, the thing holding us back is not some external barrier, it is not the job market, another person, and it is not even the situation. It is us—our unwillingness to loosen our grip on what used to be, so we cling to it because we have invested in it and have poured in time, effort, years of our life, pieces of ourselves. Somewhere along the line, we bought into the idea that if we walk away, all that investment was wasted.

That right there? That is the trap. That is what they call the sunk cost fallacy—believing you must keep investing in something just because you already have so much invested. Here is the bottom line: that time, that energy, that money, those emotions? They are already spent, they are gone and you cannot get them back—no matter how tightly you hold on or try to get them back because all you are doing now is deciding whether to keep losing more. We have all stayed in a job long past the point it stopped being a good fit or stayed in relationships where the connection was gone but the guilt was heavy or we kept chasing plans that stopped making sense because we did not want to admit they were not working. I get it, letting go feels like failure and it feels like quitting, but it is not. Not if it is done with intention and not if it is done in service of growth. The real question you must ask yourself is this: if I had not started this yet—knowing what I know now—would I choose it today? If the answer is no, then it is time to be honest about what you are holding onto—and why.

Sometimes - more often than not - we confuse loyalty with wisdom and we stick with something because we do not want to seem like we are giving up, but hear me when I say: you do not owe your past more than you owe your future. It is not disloyal to outgrow something and it is not a weakness to admit something no longer fits. What is weak is staying stuck because it is easier than facing the discomfort of letting go. Letting go does not mean what you built or tried or gave your heart to was wrong, it just means it served its purpose—and now it is time for something else. That is not failure, that is maturity. Yes, it takes guts and it takes the kind of strength most people do not get credit for because letting go means facing the unknown and it means trusting yourself enough to believe there is something better ahead—even if you cannot see it yet.

This is where everything starts to shift because when you stop basing your decisions on what you have already lost, you start basing them on what you still must gain. When you start asking not "How much have I invested?" but "Where is this taking me?"—that's when real change begins, that is when forward motion becomes possible again, and that is when you go from surviving to moving toward something meaningful. You owe it to yourself to move forward—not with guilt, fear, or out of habit, but with clarity and purpose to something better on the horizon. You must learn to trust your gut more than your history and you must trust that what you let go of was not wasted—it was part of what shaped you into someone strong enough to make better choices now. A hard truth to come to grips with is that not everything is meant to go with you - not every person, not every plan, not every version of who you used to be, because there comes a point in every journey where you have to set something down so you can pick something else up. It is in that moment—that choice— where you see the pivot point between who you were and who you are becoming. So, take a hard look at what you are still holding onto and ask yourself, "Is this carrying me, or am I carrying it?" If it is the latter, it might be time to let go and not because it did not matter—but because you do.

The Sunk Cost Fallacy

There is a story I once heard about a man who bought a fixer-upper boat (if you own one, you know BOAT stands for Bring Out Another Thousand). He poured money into that thing—replacing the motor, resealing the hull, repainting the deck and it was supposed to be a quick project, but two years later, he had spent thousands more than the boat was worth and still was not satisfied. His friends gently asked him, "Why not cut your losses and walk away?" His answer? "Because I've already put too much into it." This is the sunk cost fallacy.

We've all been there, whether it is a relationship that stopped working long ago, a job that drains us, or a business idea we keep trying to resurrect. The thought of walking away feels like failure because we have invested time, energy, love, and/or money. So, we stick with it— not because it is right, but because of what it used to mean or how much we have already given. When you reach that point, I want you to think of this brutal truth: past investment does not justify future misery.

Understanding the Fallacy

The sunk cost fallacy is when we continue a behavior or endeavor because of previously invested resources (time, money, or effort), rather than rationally evaluating whether it still serves us. It is the belief that quitting means waste, that giving up is losing, but often, staying is what truly costs us the most. This fallacy whispers to you, "Don't Walk away—you've put too much in." BUT - if you can get yourself to step back, you can see that continuing only deepens the hole. We cannot recover what is already spent, all we can do is choose wisely going forward.

When It Shows Up in Life

Think about the student who is halfway through law school, a training program, or any other type of entry level prospect and realizes they hate it. Even though they hate it, they press on—three more semesters, the bar exam, tests, practicals, etc. and then a job they dread every day they have to go in—because they have already put in so much time to the schooling and now, they have a stupid amount of loans and tuition to pay back. Or the couple who has been together ten years, emotionally distant and going through the motions, but they will not separate because "we've been through so much together" or "we have to stay together for the kids." Or maybe it is your business. You have built the brand, marketed the product, even found a customer base—but your gut keeps telling you it is not right anymore, but still, you stay because you "can't waste the years you've spent building this." And yet, the longer you stay in what is not working, the less room you make for what could be.

The Courage to Pivot Anyway

Walking away is not weakness, even if it feels like it. It is wisdom, it is taking ownership of your life rather than being owned by your past and it takes humility to admit, "This isn't it anymore." It takes maturity to say, "That season served me, but it's time to move on." Every time we free ourselves from the grip of sunk costs, we say to the world—and to ourselves—that we are worth more than just the effort we have already expended and we are worth being happy, fulfilled, and aligned. To put it in simple, everyday terms, if your GPS tells you that you are heading the wrong way, you do not keep driving just because you have already burned half a tank of gas - you turn around.

What You Do Keep

Letting go does not mean the past was worthless because every effort has taught you something, every step has built your character, and even the hard lessons shaped your intuition. You do not lose those just because you take a new road. In fact, those are the tools you take with you into the pivot and you honor the journey by being honest about where it led—and where it no longer leads.

Real World Example: Carl Jones - Security Manager and former Police Officer

Carl was born at Chanute Air Force Base in Rantoul, Illinois, the son of a U.S. Air Force sergeant and Vietnam veteran. His parents returned to California after the military, but his childhood was anything but stable, and in 1979, his father, an abusive alcoholic who Carl was a victim of was imprisoned for unspeakable crimes, and years later, died by suicide when Carl was just 17. His mother, overwhelmed by poverty and alcoholism, eventually kicked him out of the house and for a time, Carl lived in a motel with her, until permanently kicked out. He then relied on the kindness of friends like Gabe Lopez and Billy Winder, whose families took him in and gave him food, shelter, and love when he had nowhere else to turn. Carl often says their generosity is the reason he's alive today.

School was his only refuge and he thrived in academics and sports, finding discipline and camaraderie on the playing field that was absent at home but life forced him to grow up fast—he dropped out of high school a semester short of graduating when his girlfriend became pregnant. Carl later earned his GED with the intention of enlisting in the Marines, a dream he never pursued, and one of his lasting regrets. Another deep regret was being denied a role in raising his first son, who moved away with his mother and stepfather. So, determined to avoid the broken patterns of his childhood, Carl worked tirelessly to build a life of stability and purpose. He eventually became the sole guardian of his two younger sons after discovering their mother's struggles with addiction and infidelity. Juggling two jobs in retail automotive management, Carl was exhausted and barely getting by, but he refused to quit.

It was during this time that Carl met "Mark," a Pomona Police officer and K-9 handler who often bought parts for his fleet of vehicles for an off duty job. Mark's stories of law enforcement—and his appearance on the TV show *Cops*—ignited something in Carl and he knew he wanted to serve. With no clear path forward, he put himself through the extended police academy in 2000, balancing 20 hours a week of training with full-time work. Despite graduating near the top of his class, Carl faced rejection after rejection from agencies due to a past bankruptcy on his record.

Still, he refused to give up.

Carl's break came when he was hired as a reserve officer, a volunteer role that paid nothing but offered a foot in the door and it was during these early days that he met me. I would see Carl sitting in our lounge every Friday night, waiting for an officer to take him out in the field. After seeing him there on a few Fridays, I introduced myself and asked what he was doing and he explained he was waiting for an FTO trained officer to take him out into the field, but no one wanted the "new guy." Remembering what it felt like to be the new guy, I told him to grab his gear and come with me and after spending a shift in the car with him and hearing his dreams and goals and seeing the dedication and fortitude he showed, I told him he would never wait in the lounge again, and he was always welcome to ride with me. I was lucky enough to see Carl's drive and character, and was blessed to be able to step in when others overlooked him. I took him under my wing and made it my mission to not only train him in officer safety, traffic accident investigation, and SWAT tactics, but also making sure he was accepted within the department. Carl often credits me as the person who helped open the door to his dream career saying, "I would never have been hired without James," and "He believed in me when others wouldn't." But the truth of it is that Carl was a go getter who was not going to take no for an answer, I was just lucky enough to get to be a part of his journey and dream.

In 2002, Carl achieved his goal of becoming a full-time police officer at age 30 and quickly proved himself, earning a reputation as a leader and mentor. He joined the SWAT team, became an FTO, and later promoted to detective. In 2007, tragedy struck when a fellow SWAT officer—Sergio Carrera—was killed during a high-risk search warrant they were on together, a loss Carl and all of us still carry.

Carl's life expanded beyond the badge when he met Amber, who became his wife and his steadfast partner and together, they raised his two sons and, in 2009, welcomed boy-girl twins. Amber, an award-winning police dispatcher, stood beside Carl through the highs and lows of his career.

In 2016, after nearly 17 years of exemplary service, politics and toxic leadership forced an unexpected pivot. Passed over for promotion despite being first on the list and having the integrity and courage to call it out, Carl became a target of retaliatory investigations that ended with his termination in 2017. Though he fought back legally and settled out of court, his law enforcement career ended abruptly—a painful end to what he believed was his calling. This caused Carl to pivot once again, teaching criminal justice as an adjunct professor and transitioning into the private sector as a security manager while Amber also shifted careers, earning a degree in education and becoming a third-grade teacher. Together, they've built a life rooted in resilience, family, and service.

Carl's story is a testament to perseverance and reinvention. Every pivot in his life—from surviving a broken childhood to building a law enforcement career, to finding purpose again after loss—proves that resilience is not about avoiding hardship but about moving forward in the face of it. His journey reminds us that while we cannot control every storm, we can choose how we rebuild when the storm passes.

Reflective Questions to Ask Yourself

Am I staying in this because of what I hope it becomes, or because of what it really is right now? If I could go back to the beginning, knowing what I now know, would I start this again? What am I afraid will happen if I let go? What opportunities am I missing by holding onto this? Is this still serving my growth, or am I simply avoiding loss?

A Final Word

We have all heard the trite adage: "Life is short." Trite or not, it is true - time is the one commodity that when it is gone, it is gone, you are never getting it back. Life is too sacred to spend weighed down by past investments that no longer align with your future. You are not the time you have lost, the money you have spent, or the years you stayed - you are the choice you make next. Let go of what no longer serves you; not because it was not worth it—but because you are.

📓 Reflection & Action

1. What part of this chapter resonated with you most? Why?
2. What is one action you can take this week to apply a principle discussed here?
3. Are there any habits or beliefs you need to let go of to pivot successfully?
4. Who can you talk to for support or accountability around this pivot?

III

Part Three

Who You Walk With Matters – The Importance of Communication

8

8. You Do Not Have to Do It Alone — Why Your Circle Matters More Than You Think

There is one other big elephant in the room that we do not talk about enough—especially in the law enforcement world, in the military, and honestly, in any corner of life or the blue-collar world where toughness is worn like a badge of honor. We are taught to pull ourselves up by the bootstraps, to stand tall, grit our teeth, and carry on. While there is a time and place for that, let me be clear: you are not supposed to do this alone - not life, not the hard seasons, and certainly not the pivots. Yes, you have got to own your choices and yes, you have got to show up and do the work, but when you are navigating a pivot—when life throws you into the deep end, and the ground under your feet suddenly does not match the map you were using—you need people. You do not need an army of people, just a small group of the right people. Trust me, there is a difference in trying to go it alone and surrounding yourself with a group of supportive, like-minded people. I have seen people try to white-knuckle their way through a transition and when they hit a wall—mentally, physically, and/or spiritually—instead of reaching out, they doubled down. "I'll figure it out," they would say. "I just need more time. More effort. More discipline."

All that effort was not the answer because they were not failing because they were weak, they were failing because they were trying to fight a group-sized battle with a solo strategy. On the other side, I have seen the other kind - the Chris Lee's of the world. The ones who had even just one solid person in their corner, someone who reminded them they were not crazy for wanting more, someone who listened, someone who showed up and even if that person could not fix it for them, they made the weight bearable. You can guess which group came out stronger - and it is not even close.

Why Support Matters—Especially During a Pivot

Pivoting—whether it is leaving a job, retiring, starting over, or simply realizing the life you built does not quite fit anymore—is messy business, so the old rules do not apply, and the new ones have not arrived yet. You are stuck in the in-between and in that space, everything gets louder: the doubt, fear, shame, and the voice that says, "Who do you think you are to want something different?" That is not weakness, that is just the human mind doing what it does when the future is not clear. Our minds will run defense, build walls., and it will tell you stories to protect you from uncertainty. Here is where support makes all the difference, because while support does not make the hard stuff disappear, it does give you strength to face it without losing your footing. When you have someone to call or someone who will sit with you in the silence or walk you through the noise, that is not fluff - it is power. It is stability in the middle of chaos.

What the Right People Bring

The right people in your circle can give you several things: perspective when your thinking gets cloudy, courage when you start questioning your worth, accountability when your motivation falters, and even grace when you stumble—because you will stumble. No badge, title, or years of experience changes the truth that we are wired for connection and going it alone is not brave, it is avoidable suffering.

The Three Kinds of Support You will Need

This is not about leaning on one person for everything as that is too much pressure for anyone, it is about understanding that support comes in different forms—and that each form has a purpose, so let's look at some types of support to look for.

1. Emotional Support – The Steady Voices: These are the people who see you and do not flinch when you get vulnerable. They do not try to fix it, or dismiss it, or tell you it is all in your head. They just stay steady and remind you who you are when you forget. You do not need a crowd, sometimes one or two people like this is more than enough. The friend who picks up the phone every time, no matter what, the sibling who knows your story and does not try to rewrite it, or the partner who listens, even when you are not making sense. Their job is not to solve your pivot, their job is to anchor you while you walk through it.

2. Practical Support – The Hands-On Helpers: Sometimes you do not need a pep talk - you need a ride, a babysitter, or someone to sit at the kitchen table with you and go line by line through your budget. This kind of support is boots-on-the-ground, action-oriented support and it matters more than you might think. It is the friend who shows up on moving day, the neighbor who drops off dinner when you are overwhelmed, or the colleague who helps you prep for an interview. These are the people who help carry the load— not because you cannot, but because you should not have to do all

of it alone.

3. Professional Support – The Ones Who Have Been There: If you are walking unfamiliar ground—changing careers, recovering from burnout, rebuilding your life—it helps to talk to someone who has been through it. A coach, a therapist, a mentor, a retired officer who made the same leap, or a business owner who remembers what their first year felt like. A quick note of therapists......a lot of people will say that they will not talk to a therapist because "they haven't lived my life or walked in my shoes - they can't understand what I have been through." That's OK that they haven't.... they have studied the brain, trauma, stress and people's reactions to it.... they don't have to understand the nuances of the job to understand how to help.

You do not need a savior. You just need someone who is a few steps ahead, someone willing to shine a light on the trail you are walking and if you cannot find one in your immediate circle? Look outward, read, google, ask around, join a group, or listen to podcasts. Do not underestimate how much wisdom is out there—often free for the taking.

How to Build—or Rebuild—Your Circle

Now here is the uncomfortable part: most of us, dare I say all of us, are not good at asking for help and we would rather gut it out than admit we are overwhelmed. Hear me out here: you would be surprised how many people want to show up for you—if you just let them. Want to get started? Look Around, chances are, there is someone in your life who already sees you are struggling and they are just waiting for an invitation because they do not want to intrude. Do not make them guess, say, "Hey—I need a hand. Can we talk?" That is enough. Sometimes we need to fill the gaps and if you need something your current circle cannot give, that's not failure, that is life because sometimes you outgrow connections and sometimes people just are not equipped to help with what you need. That is okay, so go seek out what you need - whether it is a local meetup, reaching out to an old friend, going to therapy, or finding a mentor in your field.

Just be real, you do not need to give people the polished version of who you think they want to see - or who you want them to see. Be honest most of all and if your world feels like it is on fire, say so. Vulnerability builds trust and people connect to realness, not perfection. When the time is right, show appreciation and say thank you - a handwritten note, a phone call, a returned favor—these things matter because gratitude keeps relationships healthy. Remember to also pay it forward, offer support too, because this is not about dependence, it is about shared strength so show up for others the way you want them to show up for you.

The Power of Mentorship

A good mentor will not walk the path for you—but they will help you find your footing and they will remind you that what you are going through is not new or weird or proof that you are failing. If they are successful, they have been there, they have survived it, and maybe even stumbled harder than you have. That perspective is gold and while a mentor may not have every answer, they will help you ask better questions: What does success look like to you now? Who do you want to become—not just what do you want to do? What needs to heal before you build again? And here is the best part: one day, when the dust settles and you are standing on firmer ground, you will get to be that person for someone else.

You Are Not a Burden

Let me say this one more time for the folks in the back: asking for
help does not make you weak, it makes you brave. We live in a culture
that glorifies self-reliance—but at what cost? Burnout, loneliness, and
disconnection? Support is not a luxury; it is a lifeline and we all need it
from time to time. And let's be honest, your strength is not measured
by how much you can carry alone, it is measured by how honest you are
willing to be. How willing you are to say, "I can't do this by myself."
That is not giving up, it is leveling up.

The Unspoken Gratitude: Let Them Know They Mattered

This is a very import part of community and having those people who
walk with us. During life, we are constantly crossing paths with people
who shape us in ways they'll never realize. A teacher who believed in
you when you were a screw-up, a partner who stood by you when you
didn't deserve it, or a buddy who cracked a joke on your darkest day
and unknowingly pulled you back from the edge. This truth has been
born out in almost every class I have ever taught and asked students
about it: most of them don't know what they did and even if they did,
they do not know the ripple they left behind. We tell ourselves we'll get
around to saying "thank you," but life gets busy, pride gets in the way,
and sometimes people are gone before we ever say the words.

In a pivot, this matters more than ever, because when you're rebuilding,
you start to see just how much those connections matter—how much
of who you are came from people who poured into you, even in small
ways. Telling them what they meant isn't just about them; it's about
you, too. It is about owning your story and acknowledging the hands
that helped lift you when you didn't even know you needed lifting.

This has happened to me several times, where I have had someone come up to me that I do not recognize and they tell me they want to say thank you because I changed their lives. After speaking to them, I find out it was a call I was on where I just did my job, or gave their parents advice on how to deal with them.....to me it was just another call, just another day at work, but to them it was a life changing event because of the advice I gave or the way I handled the call. You just never know the impact you are going to have on others - and vice-versa.

Why You Should Say It Now

You never know what it means to them because sometimes people go through life wondering if they made a difference and your words might be the proof they've been looking for. Second, it can create a chain reaction because gratitude has a way of sparking something in others, and it can inspire them to keep pouring into people the way they poured into you. Finally, it can lighten your own heart because there is a kind of freedom in closing that loop, and in speaking the words that have been sitting in your chest for years.

A Challenge for You

Think of one person who impacted you—a mentor, a friend, a stranger who showed up at the right time—and tell them. A call, a letter, or a text that simply says, *"You may not realize it, but you made a difference in my life."* Don't wait for the "right time," because there isn't one. Just do it. (See my Acknowledgments section)

Real Life Example: Donny Mahoney - Retired Sheriff's Captain

When we talk about mentorship, I had the privilege of working alongside

Captain Donny Mahoney during my years with the San Bernardino County Sheriff's Department, and to this day, I count him as both a mentor and a good friend. Donny is the kind of leader you remember— not because he demanded respect, but because he earned it through quiet strength, humility, and a steady commitment to the people around him.

Before his career in law enforcement, Donny served in the United States Air Force, where he learned the discipline, work ethic, and sense of service that would define his life. The Air Force taught him that leadership is about responsibility, not recognition—about lifting others up and building trust. Those lessons carried over when he joined the San Bernardino County Sheriff's Department in 1992.

During his nearly three decades of service, Donny worked in some of the department's most demanding assignments. He served as a homicide detective, a sergeant at West Valley Detention Center, a lieutenant at the Crime Lab, and later as a captain of the largest corrections facility in the county, followed by the busiest station in the department, Rancho Cucamonga. He oversaw programs that made a tangible difference, including supporting Deputy Branden DeVault's S.T.A.R.T. program (Sheriff's Transitional Assistance Reentry Team). While he didn't create S.T.A.R.T., Donny's leadership as captain ensured the program thrived by empowering his team to succeed, as he did at every level he worked.

Donny's pivot into retirement is just as inspiring as his career. After retiring in 2021 with 29 years of dedicated service, he didn't fade into the background—he pivoted into a new chapter of life with the same focus and energy that made him an exceptional captain. He stays active, playing golf and pickle ball, and travels the world with his wife, making the most of every season of life. What strikes me most is that Donny didn't stumble into this comfortable and fulfilling retirement—he planned for it.

Donny always lived within his means. He didn't carry debt, and he invested wisely, making sure his future was as secure as the teams he led. Financial freedom, for Donny, isn't about wealth for its own sake; it's about freedom—the ability to step away from a demanding career and still have the health, stability, and resources to enjoy life with the people who matter most. His story perfectly ties into the principles I share in the financial planning chapter of The Pivot: the idea that stability and foresight are forms of freedom. Donny is living proof that the decisions you make with your money—just like the pivots you make in your career—shape the life you get to enjoy later.

When I see Donny now, traveling, staying active, and enjoying this season with his wife, I'm reminded that a pivot isn't just about moving away from something—it's about moving toward something better. He built a career on service, but he also built a life that would give him the freedom to enjoy the fruits of his hard work when the time came. I could not be more proud that Donny is a part of my circle.

Final Word: Build Your Circle with Intention

If you take nothing else from this chapter, let it be this: you do not have to have it all figured out before you deserve support. You do not need to be "ready" and you do not need to earn it. You are human and that is enough, so start small: make the call, send the text, schedule the meeting, or ask someone, "Can I run something by you?" And when you find your circle—whether it is one person or five—nurture it, protect it, and pour into it because the strength of your support system will determine the strength of your pivot.

You are not weak for needing people, you are wise for choosing the right ones.

📕 Reflection & Action

1. What part of this chapter resonated with you most? Why?
2. What is one action you can take this week to apply a principle discussed here?
3. Are there any habits or beliefs you need to let go of to pivot successfully?
4. Who can you talk to for support or accountability around this pivot?

9

9. Say What Needs to Be Said — Communicating Through Change

Every pivot, every major life shift, comes with a conversation. Some-times, it is a conversation you have alone with your own reflection in the mirror and other times, it is a series of conversations — with your partner, your boss, your parents, your children, or even old friends who no longer feel like the same people. Change is not just internal and it demands that you *say* something, because it requires you to step into a moment of vulnerability, uncertainty, and risk. You cannot pivot well without honest communication.

The Weight of Unspoken Words

Staying silent might feel easier in the moment and maybe you tell yourself that people will not understand, or it is not the time, or even that things will work themselves out. I get that silence feels safe and it feels like you are protecting yourself and others, but silence in a season of change is like stepping onto a bridge and refusing to tell anyone else where you are going. You are carrying a secret map, but no one else knows the route., so no one can meet you halfway. The danger of silence is not just that it isolates you, it also slows your growth as unspoken words become weights that linger, heavy and unseen, until they seep out sideways — into your stress, your sleep, your health, your mood, your relationships.

Imagine a glass of water and each unspoken feeling, each withheld truth, is a pebble dropped in. At first, the ripples are small, but soon, the glass is full. It overflows and the pressure inside builds until it bursts in an unexpected way — anger, withdrawal, exhaustion, resentment. The people around you might not know the full story, but they will see the effects, so if you want to pivot well, you owe it to yourself — and to those who matter — to say what needs to be said.

What Courageous Communication Looks Like

Courageous communication is not about drama or confrontation and it is not a weapon or a fight, nor is it a performance or a battle cry. It is about clarity, respect, and truth and it is about choosing connection over assumption, and movement over resentment. When you are in the middle of a pivot — that uncertain, messy place — courageous communication might look like:

- "This isn't working for me anymore."
- "I need something different, and I'm not sure what that looks like yet."
- "I've changed, and I know that might be hard to hear."
- "I want to be honest with you, even if it's uncomfortable."

It does not have to be eloquent. It just must be *real*.

My Hardest Conversation

When my shoulder injuries and heart issues made it clear I could not continue my career in law enforcement, I had to have one of the hardest conversations of my life. I sat down with my wife down and said plainly: "I think it's finally time." Those words felt heavy, because we both knew what that meant — a loss of a career and a good income, possible financial uncertainty, and a future that did not necessarily look like what was planned. But saying it aloud gave us something critical: a place to start and the storm in my head became something we could face together and while that moment was not easy, and it was not perfect, it was *necessary*. Change does not just require action — it requires alignment. And alignment starts with words.

How to Communicate During a Pivot

If you are reading this, you might know that your pivot demands a conversation that scares you, or maybe you have been avoiding it, so here are a few guiding principles that can help you navigate these conversations with courage and care:

1. Speak Early, Not Perfectly - Waiting for the perfect moment or the perfect words is a trap. It is often silence that breeds misunderstanding and resentment, so if something needs to be said, say it early—before the pressure builds, before assumptions set in. Try opening with something simple like: "I've been thinking about something important, and I want to talk it through." This signals respect, honesty, and intention. You do not have to have every answer, you just must start.

2. Use "I" Statements, Not Accusations - this can be a tough one.... trust me. Pivots are personal and the changes you are making can feel like criticism or rejection to others if framed poorly, so speak from your own experience. Do your best to avoid blame or over-

generalizations, so instead of: "You never support me," Try: "I've been feeling unsupported lately, and I want us to figure this out together." This opens the door for collaboration instead of defensiveness.

3. Invite Dialogue, Not Just Declaration - Your pivot affects others, so invite their voice. Ask: "How does that land with you?" or "What do you need from me as we go through this?" or "What's your perspective on this change?" Dialogue builds bridges and turns a one-way announcement into a shared journey.

4. Prepare for Discomfort - Just because you choose to communicate does not mean everyone will respond how you hope. Some will resist, some will misunderstand, some may pull away, but that is normal. It does not mean you were wrong to speak, it just means change is hard—for all of us, so prepare your heart to hold the discomfort, knowing that honest communication often shakes the foundation before building it stronger.

5. Revisit the Conversation as You Grow - One conversation is rarely enough, so as your pivot unfolds, circle back and check in, clarify, and speak again because change is not a moment — it is a season and seasons require ongoing conversation.

Look Them in the Eye, and Tell the Truth

You do not have to shout and you do not have to make a speech, you just must tell the truth—plainly, respectfully, and with the kind of calm that comes from knowing your soul is finally in alignment. Sometimes the most radical act in the middle of a pivot is simply: "Here is where I am. Here is where I am going. I hope you will walk with me—but I am going either way." That is not abandonment, it is honesty, maturity, and leadership.

The Power of Vulnerability in Communication

To say what needs to be said, you will have to be vulnerable and that is often the hardest part because vulnerability means risking rejection or misunderstanding. It means exposing your fears and hopes, but it is also where true connection is born because when you show up vulnerable, you invite others to do the same and that creates a space where transformation is possible.

What Happens When You Do Not Say What Needs to Be Said

Avoiding tough conversations does not make them disappear, it just lets problems fester until they burst. I have seen relationships crumble, careers stall, and dreams die because no one said the hard things when they should have and not communicating during a pivot is like driving blindfolded — you do not know what is ahead, and the damage you cause can be permanent.

Practical Tips for Saying What Needs to Be Said

- Write it out first. Sometimes the hardest part is organizing your thoughts. Write a letter to yourself or the other person. You do not have to send it; just get your truth on paper.
- Practice with a trusted friend or counselor. Role-play the conversation to gain confidence.
- Choose the right time and place. Find a moment free from distractions and tension.
- Breathe. Center yourself before speaking.
- Listen as much as you speak. Communication is a two-way street.

When Communication Feels Impossible

Sometimes, even when you try, communication breaks down and if someone refuses to listen or meet you halfway, that is their choice — not a reflection of your worth or your right to be heard. In those moments, keep speaking your truth to yourself and seek other outlets: journals, support groups, mentors.

Remember: Your voice matters. Your story matters.

Real World Example: Jason Hendrix - Retired Sergeant

In talking about communication, I thought of Jason. Never one to shy away from confrontation or be afraid to speak up for what it right, I have known Sergeant Jason Hendrix for a long time—since 2009, to be exact. Over the years, I've seen what kind of man and leader he is, not just from the badge he wears, but from the way he shows up when things get hard. Jason is not the kind of person who leads for recognition; he leads because he believes in the mission. When he co-founded the Cannonball Memorial Run, I knew I wanted to be a part of it. I became a board member in its second year, and to this day, I count that decision as one of the most meaningful pivots of my own life.

Jason's story is filled with the kind of moments that test everything you are. Early in his career, in March 1996, he found himself in the middle of a violent confrontation while off duty in Palm Desert. He stepped in to protect innocent people and ended up in a shootout. A bullet struck him in the head and multiple other spots - he was shot 8 times. Most people wouldn't walk away from that, but Jason did and instead of letting the experience define him with fear or bitterness, he used it to sharpen his sense of purpose. He often said that moment reminded him that life is fragile and that service demands more than just courage—it demands heart.

In 1999, Jason survived yet another life-altering event when he was aboard a sheriff's helicopter that crashed into a fog-shrouded mountain during a response call. He and two other deputies were stranded for over 12 hours before they were rescued. Experiences like that don't just leave scars; they leave a mark on who you are and again, Jason didn't just walk away from that crash—he walked forward, with a renewed determination to make his work matter.

Jason promoted through the ranks and finished his career as a Sergeant with the San Bernardino County Sheriff's Department in October 2022, but his impact reaches far beyond the department. When the ambushes of police officers began making national headlines, Jason refused to sit back and watch, so he co-founded Cannonball Memorial Run, a mission to honor fallen officers and provide immediate financial relief to their families. It wasn't about publicity; it was about standing in the gap when a family's world falls apart.

Standing beside Jason during those long Cannonball runs, watching the miles roll by and hearing the names of fallen officers, I saw how his vision was fueled by something personal—an understanding of pain, loss, and survival. He took his own near-death experiences and turned them into something bigger than himself.

Jason's story is the perfect example of what I mean when I talk about pivots. Twice, life handed him moments that could have ended everything. Twice, he walked away stronger. But he didn't stop there— he used his survival to build something that helps others, something that ensures no family is left behind in their darkest moment.

Final Thoughts: Build Bridges with Your Voice

The voice you use during a pivot shapes the road ahead, so let it be honest, human, YOURS. People cannot meet you where you are if they do not know where you are, so say what needs to be said—even if your voice shakes because that is how bridges are built, how alignment begins, and how transformation takes root.

📒 Reflection & Action

1. What part of this chapter resonated with you most? Why?
2. What is one action you can take this week to apply a principle discussed here?
3. Are there any habits or beliefs you need to let go of to pivot successfully?
4. Who can you talk to for support or accountability around this pivot?

10

10. Navigating Personal Relationships Through the Pivot

While the prior two chapters dealt with building your circle and communicating honestly, this chapter is going to delve deeper into navigating those relationships. Change does not happen in a vacuum. It might start with a decision you make alone—quitting a job, starting something new, moving cities, or setting a boundary—but the effects ripple out and the first place those ripples hit tend to be our relationships. Your pivot does not just change your path, it changes the way you walk alongside others—and whether they choose to keep walking with you. It can be tough, sometimes it is heartbreaking, but oftentimes, it is extremely clarifying.

Some people will grow with you, while some will not. Some will rise to meet your new season, while others will quietly (or loudly) resist the shift. A friend of mine's wife, Carol, has a saying, "When people reveal themselves to you, trust them." If they show you, they are not on board with your pivot and it does not seem to be coming from a place of love or support, or even constructive criticism, maybe it is time to take a hard look at that relationship, because it may be time to cut that out of your life. That is not a failure, that is a fact. Every serious life transition—whether it is a career change, a spiritual awakening, a move, a decision to finally deal with your past—presses up against the relational frameworks around you and those frameworks either stretch to accommodate the new you or snap under pressure. It is not always just about who stays and who goes, it is about how you relate, how you communicate, and how you honor yourself and others through the process.

Here is what I have learned after decades of witnessing people face change under pressure not only on the job, but in my own family, and in my own life: Strong, healthy relationships will not hold you back: they will challenge you to rise, they will speak hard truths, they will walk through the unknown with you, but you cannot expect to hold onto those relationships—much less grow them—without intention.

What does that look like?

Step One: Communicate Clearly and Early - A lot of tension in relationships during a pivot does not come from what is changing—it comes from silence, assumptions, and from confusion. You are in motion and thinking big and this can make you uncertain or energized or afraid and people around you are watching from the outside, trying to guess what is happening. Do not make them guess and let people in. You do not have to broadcast every insecurity or plan to that world, but the people closest to you—your spouse, your kids, your parents, your best friends—deserve clarity. Tell them what is changing, why it matters to you, and how it might affect them.

When I transitioned out of law enforcement, I wasn't great at this.... we talked about it, sure. But with the daily rigors of life, I did not spend nearly enough time communicating with my wife about what the change would look like. We kind of went from one day I was leaving for work, and the next day I was home. It took some time to find the rhythm and get into a new groove, so I am urging you to not make the mistake I did. Bring your spouse into the fold and do not wait for her to feel like she is being left behind.

If your pivot is going to impact your schedule, your availability, your finances, or your mood—talk about it. Not from a place of defensiveness and I will tell you from personal experience, this has been my kryptonite…. for some reason, when it comes to my spouse, at times I can get very defensive and that is something I am still working on, because she deserves better from me. So, listen to me when I say, come to the conversation from a place of respect - you are not asking for permission, you are giving them the gift of understanding where you are coming from and you are building trust. That trust becomes the safety net when the growing pains hit and while clarity might not make everyone happy, it will give them a choice: to meet you where you are or to ask for what they need in return.

Step Two: Expect Resistance

Here is something no one likes to admit: Even the people who love you can struggle with your growth because your change is a mirror, and it can reflect other's stagnation, fears, or unresolved dreams. When you start making moves, it shines a light on the places they have stood still. Take note, that does not make them bad people, it makes them human because not everyone grows at the same pace. You might be leaving behind old habits, old coping mechanisms, even old roles in your relationships and some people are going to take that personally.

They will say you've "changed." (You have.) They will say you are different. (You are.) They might even question your motives. (Stay grounded.) Growth has a cost and one of the most painful tolls is being misunderstood by people you love but hear me on this: You are not responsible for their comfort; you are responsible for your alignment. Remember to keep compassion and grace close and do not harden your heart, as resistance often comes from fear—fear of being left, fear of losing intimacy, or fear of not recognizing the person you are becoming.

So, meet it with both clarity and compassion: "This is new for both of us," "I value our relationship, even if some things are changing," "I'm not leaving you—I'm becoming more of who I am." These conversations will stretch you as a person, but they are worth it because the alternative is isolation, and no dream is worth achieving if it costs you every person who ever mattered to you.

Step Three: Redefine Your Inner Circle

This ties into chapter 8 - every pivot sharpens your vision and with clearer vision, you start seeing relationships for what they are—not what you hoped they would be, so identify YOUR people. Look at your current circle and ask yourself: Who encourages you without enabling your excuses? Who sees your potential, not just your past? Who pushes you toward growth, not comfort?

Those are your people, and it is not always the loudest voices or the longest relationships, sometimes it is the quiet presence who shows up consistently and sometimes it is the new friend who asks you tough questions and believes in your answers. Just because someone has been in your life a long time does not mean they deserve front-row access today because longevity does not equal loyalty, and closeness does not equal connection. You want relationships that bring depth—that anchor you in purpose, truth, and grace, so give yourself permission to shift roles. You do not have to cut everyone off, but you do have to re-calibrate and reassess your circle and some relationships will move from the spotlight to the background—and that is okay. Honor them for what they were and release them if they no longer align and build your circle around the life you are trying to live, not the one you have outgrown.

Step Four: Anchor Key Relationships

While some relationships will shift, others are non-negotiable because they are your roots and even in change, they deserve to be protected, nurtured, and fought for.

Your Partner: If you are married, dating seriously, or in a long-term partnership, your pivot is not just yours, as it affects your schedules, your routines, your stress levels, and sometimes your identity as a couple. So, it is especially important to stay connected: check in often—not just about logistics, but about emotions, make time for intimacy and fun, not just strategy, and reassure each other of your shared future. It is easy to get so focused on where you are going that you forget to look beside you, but if you lose your partner's presence along the way, the destination will not feel like home when you get there.

Your Kids: Kids feel everything, even when they cannot name it and they will notice the tension, the new energy, the tired nights, and the shifting priorities. Talk to them and use simple, honest language to explain what is changing, reassure them that they are loved, secure, and not forgotten, and keep routines consistent where you can. Do not wait until you "have it all figured out" to show up emotionally. You need to show them what healthy growth looks like—in progress, in imperfection, and with presence.

Your Close Friends: The real ones will try, but even they need your attention, send the text, make the call, and say thank you for their patience and their presence. They are the ones who remember who you were before the pivot and still believe in who you are becoming, so nurture those connections because loyalty without communication eventually becomes distance.

Step Five: Let Go with Grace

Some relationships will not make it through the pivot and maybe they were not built to. Maybe they had an expiration date, or maybe you have just changed in ways they cannot accept. Do not beat yourself up or feel guilty as this does not make you a villain - it makes you honest. So how do you know it is time to step back from a relationship? Here are a couple of suggestions to look for: you feel emotionally drained after every interaction, they only support the version of you that stays small or predictable, or your goals are met with eye rolls, silence, or sabotage. You do not need enemies to derail your growth, sometimes all it takes is the quiet disapproval of someone you once trusted and when you discover that, it is time to make a cut.

Honor the Role They Played

Not every relationship is meant for every season, but that does not mean it was a waste, because some people come into your life to walk you through a single chapter—not the whole book. Let go without resentment, but do not keep returning out of guilt or nostalgia. You do not have to burn bridges, but you do not have to keep crossing ones that do not lead where you are going.

Final Thoughts: Grow Together or Grow Apart

I am not going to sugarcoat it—your pivot is going to test your relation-ships. It is going to challenge your communication, and it is going to expose assumptions. It is going to make you reevaluate the very fabric of your support system, but here is the gift at the end: It will also deepen the right relationships. It will help you build a tribe of people who love you not for who you were, but for who you are becoming. These are the people who do not flinch when you dream big, do not pull away when you struggle, and do not disappear when life gets messy.

Those people? They are worth everything, so embrace them and hold them close, because they do not just survive your pivot, they strengthen it. The pivot is not just about finding your next step; it is about finding your people for the road ahead. So, communicate clearly, hold space for others' feelings, stay grounded in your truth, and do not be afraid to walk forward with a smaller but stronger circle. Change is coming so bring the people who help you walk it with grace.

📕 Reflection & Action

1. What part of this chapter resonated with you most? Why?
2. What is one action you can take this week to apply a principle discussed here?
3. Are there any habits or beliefs you need to let go of to pivot successfully?
4. Who can you talk to for support or accountability around this pivot?

IV

Part Four

Practical Resilience

11. Financial Planning for Life Changes — Stability Is a Form of Freedom

Let us talk about something that often gets pushed aside when we start talking about change: money. It is a huge factor for all of us - especially if you have retired and will be on a fixed income. We love the emotional side of a pivot— "follow your dreams," "trust the process," "bet on yourself." All that is important, no doubt, but let us not kid ourselves— dreams without dollars can turn into stress quickly. While change is emotional, it is also logistical and the one thing that can either stabilize or sabotage your pivot is how you handle your finances. Now, this is not about being rich, it is about being ready and about having a grip on your situation, even if that grip feels a little shaky at first. It is about building a life that is not held together by duct tape and prayer alone, because I have seen people with big hearts and big visions fall apart simply because they did not pause to look at the numbers. I have also seen others—some with half the resources—make moves with strength and purpose because they built a financial foundation first.

Stability is a form of freedom because it lets you breathe; let's you say yes to opportunity without spiraling into anxiety and lets you walk away from what is not working without being shackled to it by fear. Let us build that kind of stability.

A Good Financial Plan Does Four Things

We are not talking about rocket science here. A solid plan with your money is not about knowing the stock market inside and out, it is about building structure in the prep for the pivot and if you do it right, your financial plan will do four important things: A sound plan will keep you from reacting out of fear as fear-based decisions usually come with a price tag. A good plan gives you breathing room so you can respond instead of reacting. It gives structure to uncertainty because when everything else feels like it is changing, your financial plan can be a constant. It grounds you and gives you peace of mind. It opens doors that might otherwise stay closed because you have a cushion, you have options—and options are powerful in a pivot. It builds confidence that you can do hard things. Watching yourself take charge of your money builds belief in your ability to take charge of your life. So, let's break down how to get there—step by step.

Step 1: Take Inventory- Here is where most people want to turn the other way and run, but if you want to gain control of your financial future, you must get brutally honest about your present, so pull out a notebook or open a spreadsheet and ask yourself these questions: What do I own? I am talking about savings, checking, retirement, investments, vehicles, property—anything with real value. What do I owe? Here we are talking mortgage. Car loan. Credit card debt. Student loans. That money you "borrowed" from your parents and have not paid back yet. List it all. What is coming in? What is going out? Add up your income from all sources, then write down every recurring expense. Include the subscriptions you forgot you had, the gym membership you do not use, and the fast food you grab out of habit. This part stings a little—but it is also freeing because once you know the lay of the land, you are no longer walking blind and the truth of this is: you cannot fix what you will not face - or what you do not know.

Step 2: Create Two Budgets: A pivot usually comes in two phases: survival and growth, which is why I recommend building two budgets.

1. Survival Budget - This is your lean plan and covers only the basics—what you need to get by while you are in transition. Think: rent/mortgage, utilities, food, gas, insurance, minimum payments on debts. Everything else is negotiable during this phase and is not about punishment, it is about buying yourself time and space to move through the pivot without spiraling into debt or panic.

2. Growth Budget - Once things start to stabilize, you pivot into growth mode and now you begin adding in what helps you move forward: debt repayment beyond minimums, retirement contributions, skill development, travel or relocation savings, investing in your new direction. The survival budget gets you through, while the growth budget builds your future. Both have a place, both require discipline, and both remind you that this season is not forever—but how you handle it will shape what comes next.

Step 3: Cut Emotionally, Not Just Logically - we have all heard the financial gurus say, "Just cut unnecessary spending." Sounds simple enough, right? Here is what they do not tell you: spending is not always logical, it is emotional, because sometimes the things we spend money on are not about luxury, they are about identity, comfort, or belonging. That overpriced coffee? It might be the only thing in your day that feels "normal." The subscription box you never use might just be tied to a version of yourself you are not ready to let go of yet, so instead of just slashing things based on numbers, ask a deeper question: Does this expense support the life I am building now? That is the filter. That is the lens to look at every expense through. Not "Can I afford this?" but "Does this expense line up with the version of me I'm becoming?" Cutting spending does not mean cutting joy. It means cutting distractions.

Step 4: Build a Cushion—Start Small - Let me tell you something I have learned the hard way: life will throw you a curve-ball. It could be a flat tire, a medical bill, or a job that vanishes overnight and when the curve comes, having even a small cushion can make the difference between a crisis and a detour. You do not need ten grand in savings right out of the gate, you just need a starting point and even $500 tucked away gives you breathing room. Breathing room is priceless when the pressure is on, so start with what you can even if it's just ten bucks a week extra from a side hustle, or even that tax refund you were going to blow on a gadget you will forget about in two months. Your goal is progress, not perfection and every dollar you save says, "I believe in my future more than my impulse."

Step 5: Talk to Someone You Trust - You do not have to do this alone and in fact, you should not. I have used my dad as a financial sounding board my whole life because of the example he set. Money is one of those things we have been taught to keep quiet about, but in this instance, you cannot afford to. Find someone who has walked this road ahead of you who is financially solid, emotionally grounded, and willing to listen without judgment. Maybe it is a friend, a financial coach, a pastor, a parent, or a retired mentor. Someone who will tell you the truth and remind you that this season does not define you. So, ask for help, get perspective, and be willing to learn, because when your pride is louder than your progress, you lose every time.

Do not Let Pride Block Your Progress

Let me speak plainly for a second - Pride (remember our chapter on EGO) has ruined more financial futures than poverty ever could, because too many people pretend they are fine while the bank account says otherwise. They drive cars they cannot afford to impress people they do not like and swipe credit cards instead of having hard conversations and when the debt catches up or the income dries up, they crumble. There was a commercial in the 90's where a woman was talking about the neighbors and said, "The Jones have such a big house and a new car and a new boat - however do they do it?" And the camera pans to Mr. Jones in his backyard and he says, "We're in debt up to our eyeballs!" That is not what you want - stop trying to impress other people with your "stuff." There is no shame in starting over, just as there is no shame in asking for help or admitting that you need to pivot your finances, just like you are pivoting your life. You are not falling behind the Jones, you are laying a better foundation and that takes courage—not just strategy.

Budget Like a Builder

Think of money like any other tool in your toolbox, as it does what YOU tell it to do. If you do not give it direction, it will disappear into the cracks of life—snacks, subscriptions, late fees, coffees, and upgrades you did not need. But if you treat it with respect—if you budget like a builder—you will start to build something steady. You start to build peace, options, and the kind of life where you do not have to say yes to jobs, relationships, or situations that drain you just because you are broke. That is freedom, real freedom and while it may not be flashy, or always fun, it is worth it in the long haul because at the end of your pivot it will all pay off.

The Payoff of Financial Discipline

You will not always see the results right away; in fact, very rarely will you see immediate results. It can be frustrating, especially in a world obsessed with instant everything but financial discipline is like working out or eating right. It takes time as it builds strength quietly, slowly, and consistently until one day you realize you are sleeping better because the bills are paid, you are not afraid to check your bank account, you can say yes to an opportunity without panicking, and you can say no to a bad fit without fear of missing out on the money you thought you needed.

That is the real win, and it is not just about money, it is about agency. You are not just surviving anymore, you are choosing and choice, my friend, is powerful.

Real World Story: Aram Choe - Lieutenant / Podcaster / LEO Ambassador

I first met Aram during his participation in the Cannonball Memorial Run, where the air is heavy with stories of sacrifice and service. Aram wasn't there to be noticed—he was there because the mission mattered, and that is something you can feel when you're around him: a quiet strength, the kind that doesn't need to shout to be heard.

Aram's career began in 1999, when he started as a Deputy Sheriff Trainee with the Los Angeles County Sheriff's Department and more than 24 years later, he serves as a Lieutenant with the ElMonte Police Department, but the path between those two points has been anything but linear. Law enforcement has a way of forcing pivots on its people— changes in responsibility, perspective, and even purpose. Aram has faced those moments head-on, adapting each time by choosing to lead with intention rather than just following routine.

One of his most defining pivots came when he realized that leadership wasn't just about what happened in the field, but how effectively you could communicate under pressure. That realization led him to pursue higher education and eventually earn a Master's degree in Administrative Public Relations. Today, he teaches strategic communication as an adjunct professor at California Baptist University, showing future leaders how the words they choose and the messages they send can shape trust, build resilience, and inspire action.

Aram didn't stop there. He created the 911Strong Podcast, a platform that connects first responders, community leaders, and listeners who want to understand the realities of public safety. When the podcast debuted, it quickly climbed into Apple's top 200—proof that his voice resonated well beyond the department walls. Aram is also a consistent presence on social media, promoting officer wellness, jiu jitsu, and financial well being through investing.

What makes Aram's story so fitting for The Pivot is his understanding that careers—and life—are never static. He's learned to shift roles without losing his sense of mission, moving from front line operations to mentorship and public engagement. Whether he's speaking on national television, coaching a rookie officer, or teaching a classroom of future leaders, Aram stays grounded in the belief that service is about leaving things better than you found them.

As I have said about several of the examples, his journey is a powerful example of how the right pivot isn't always about stepping away from who you are, but stepping deeper into what you're meant to do. Aram is a man of faith, integrity, and honor and I count it as a blessing to call him my friend.

Final Word: You Are the Builder

At the end of the day, this is not about being perfect with your finances, it is about being intentional and recognizing that your pivot does not just need passion, it just needs a plan. Money is a necessary and critical part of that plan, so take inventory, create your two budgets, cut what does not serve the life you are building, build a cushion, seek wise counsel and walk this thing out with clarity. Remember, stability is not just nice to have—it is necessary, because it is what keeps your pivot steady when the emotions run high, and the road gets rough. It is what allows you to say "yes" when opportunity knocks and "no" when compromise calls. As former SEAL commander Jocko Willink would say, "Discipline equals freedom."

Freedom gives you room to become who you were meant to be. So, budget like a builder, live like a leader, and pivot like someone who is not just chasing a dream—but laying the foundation to sustain it.

📓 Reflection & Action

1. What part of this chapter resonated with you most? Why?
2. What is one action you can take this week to apply a principle discussed here?
3. Are there any habits or beliefs you need to let go of to pivot successfully?
4. Who can you talk to for support or accountability around this pivot?

12

12. Standing in the Fire: Resilience Under Criticism and Public Failure

Let's talk about something few of us ever prepare for: what happens when the world is watching, and you fail - not just quietly fail or have a bad day or drop the ball in private, I am talking about a misstep—real or perceived—that plays out under scrutiny, judgment, and the opinions of people who don't know you, haven't walked your path, and sure as hell wouldn't hold up under the same pressure. If you've spent any amount of time in the public eye—whether as a first responder, a leader, a teacher, or just someone people look to—you know this truth: **you are never just allowed to fail.** Your mistakes are rarely yours alone and they become headlines, water cooler gossip, benchmarks for other people's opinions, rumor and innuendo. And that weight? It can crush you if you're not ready for it.

I've seen it destroy good men and women, and not because they did something so egregious, but because they were caught in a moment of human error—something everyone does—but with eyes on them, it became something else. Once the tide turns, it is hard to stop the current, and I want to talk to you about that - about standing in the fire, and what it means to get knocked flat where everyone can see it, and how to get back up without losing yourself in the process.

When Reputation Is Your Currency

In law enforcement, the military, or any role of high responsibility, your reputation is your most valuable asset. We spend decades building it—one decision, one report, one mission at a time, and your integrity, your word, how you carry yourself, how you respond under pressure—it all becomes part of the story people tell about you. You spend years building trust and when something goes sideways? I have often heard it referred to as a bank account - you are building your "trust" account day by day - and just like a real account, that takes time. Occasionally you will have to make a withdrawl, and that is ok, but when you really screw up publicly - especially if it is an issue of trust or integrity, you will go bankrupt in the trust account. That reputation becomes the battlefield, but let me be clear here because sometimes the criticism is warranted. Sometimes we screw up, get too comfortable, too confident, or we let ego drive instead of humility. Trust me, I have made decisions I regretted, I've lost my temper, I've carried out orders that deep down I wasn't so sure about - not that they were illegal orders, I just did not agree with the order because I knew better. We're human and we are gonna screw up - but is it a mistake of the heart or a mistake of the brain? If you forgot something, that is one thing….it is a training issue to fix, but if it is a mistake of the heart and you truly knew better and knew what you were doing was dishonest, that is a whole different game.

Other times the criticism comes from may come from misunderstandings, from political agendas, from people who weren't there, or from Monday-morning quarterbacks who've never run a code-3 call, made a death notification, or stood between a victim and a violent threat. When that spotlight hits you, it doesn't always matter if you were right, it matters what people think. There is an old saying that may be a bit trite, but generally holds true, and that is that perception is reality, and the truth is, you can be 100% right and still lose in the court of public opinion.

That's a hard pill to swallow.

The Shame Spiral

Public failure doesn't just bruise your ego—it cuts deep into your identity because it whispers things like: "You're not who you thought you were," "They were right about you," or "You'll never recover from this." That's the shame spiral, and it is not the event itself that takes us out—it's what we *tell ourselves* afterward. Shame thrives in silence, in secrecy and it wraps itself around your self-worth and squeezes. The worst part of that is when you are the one in the arena, when you're carrying the weight of the badge, or the rank, or the leadership title, you're trained to project strength, stoicism, and competence. Because of this, you suffer in silence, and you keep showing up, smiling through the fire, while inside you're crumbling.

Let me say this clearly: failure does not mean you're a fraud, it means you're human, and being human in a system that sometimes forgets that is a radical act of courage.

The Psychology of Public Collapse

Let's look at what happens to the mind when failure goes public. Psychologists refer to this kind of experience as "identity threat under scrutiny." It occurs when your sense of self—how you see yourself and how others see you—collide in a painful, dissonant way, and here is what typically follows:

1. Hypervigilance — You become obsessed with how people see you, and you scan every room, every conversation, trying to gauge who believes in you and who doesn't.
2. Withdrawal — You isolate, not because you don't need support, but because you don't want to burden people or admit that you're hurting.
3. Self-sabotage — You stop showing up fully, and you pull back from the work you love, or you numb out with distractions or self-punishment and stop believing you deserve better.
4. Identity confusion — You begin to question everything. "Who am I without the badge? Who am I now that people see me differently?"

This is the invisible part of public failure and the part we rarely talk about. I have lived it, and I have walked beside people who lived it too and what I have learned is, you will not heal by hiding. You will only heal by walking through the middle of the fire—head high, heart open.

Accountability and Grace

Now let me balance this out, because I'm not here to tell you that all criticism is unfounded or unfair. Sometimes we do need to be held accountable because sometimes we were wrong. But here's where I draw the line: Accountability is not annihilation, and you can own your mistake without being destroyed by it. You can learn from it without becoming it, and you can apologize, repair, and grow—without giving up your entire identity. What makes us resilient isn't perfection, it is the willingness to stand in truth, to own what's yours, and to let go of what isn't. To say: "Yes, I made that call—and here's what I've learned" or "Yes, I could've done that better—and I take full responsibility" or "No, I'm not going to carry your projection of who I am just because it makes you more comfortable." That takes backbone - and grace—for yourself and for others.

You Are Not the Story They Tell About You

Here's the part you need to write on your heart in indelible ink - you are not your worst moment, you are not your last headline, and you are not the story being told about you in rooms you've never entered.

You are who you choose to become in the aftermath.

I've seen men publicly ridiculed for doing what they believed was right, and I have seen officers disciplined for decisions made in seconds, under conditions no civilian would survive. I've seen fathers, mentors, community leaders—good men—turned into scapegoats because someone needed a fall guy, and I have seen those same men and women rebuild, reinvent, and reclaim their narrative. You get to do that too.

Redemption Isn't a Clean Line

Let me be honest: recovery from public failure isn't linear because one day you're fine, and the next you're back in your head, replaying the moment it all went sideways. Some people will never see you the same way, some doors will close, and some opportunities may dry up. That is ok and that is real life, but other things will open: doors you never expected, friendships built on truth instead of image, a deeper sense of self, and a quieter kind of confidence.

There is life after the fall—but you've got to be brave enough to climb out of the rubble and start walking again, even if no one claps, and even if no one comes with you, you walk because redemption is not about making everyone else believe in you again. It's about believing in yourself—especially when others don't.

Calloused but Not Closed

Here's the trick: let the experience callous you, like the skin on your fingertips and palms after years of swinging a hammer—but don't let it close you. You'll be tempted to harden up, to shut down and say, "Screw it. I'll never put myself out there again."

Don't.

We need men and women in this world who have been through the fire and came out refined, not ruined. The world needs your scars, your wisdom, and your grit because someone else is watching, and that someone else is going to need your story to survive their own.

You want to know the real pivot? It's this: moving from shame to service. From "What will they think of me?" to "Who can I help with what I've learned?"

That's where the power is. That's where the healing is.

My Own Reckoning

I will not sit here and pretend I have not made mistakes because I have made a mountain of them. I have had cases I wish I handled differently, people I failed to support the way I should have, and moments where

I said too much—or didn't speak up when I should've. And yes, I've been talked about, misunderstood, and criticized. Sometimes justly, sometimes unfairly, but I made a decision a long time ago: I will not be defined by whispers, and I will not let people who haven't lived my life decide the value of my journey. I will keep showing up—with humility, yes—but also with strength, and I will keep telling the truth, because someone out there needs to know that surviving the fire is possible.

Closing the Chapter

If you've faced public failure and been dragged, doubted, dismissed, or demonized, let me tell you: You are not done, you are not broken beyond repair, and you are not unworthy of love, respect, or a second act. You may and probably will always carry the weight of what happened but you now also carry wisdom, perspective, and the kind of quiet power that can only be forged in the dark. Use it. Use it to mentor someone, to write your story, to lead with compassion, or to build something new.

And the next time someone tells you who you are, look them in the eye, smile, and say: "That's who I was. Let me introduce you to who I've become."

📔 Reflection & Action

1. Have you ever experienced a moment of public embarrassment or failure? What impact did it have on your identity?
2. What stories are you still telling yourself about that failure—and are they true?
3. Where might you be carrying shame that needs to be released?
4. What would it look like to reclaim your story on your terms?

5. Who needs to hear your experience—not your perfection, but your resilience?

13

13. Learning from Setbacks — What Failure Really Teaches You

One of my favorite quotes is from a speech given by Theodore Roosevelt at the Sorbonne, in Paris, France on April 23, 1910: "It is not the critic who counts, not the one who points out how the strong man stumbled or how the doer of deeds might have done them better. The credit belongs to the man who is actually in the arena, whose face is marred with sweat and dust and blood; who strives valiantly; who errs and comes short again and again; who knows the great enthusiasms, the great devotions, and spends himself in a worthy cause; who, if he wins, knows the triumph of high achievement; and who, if he fails, at least fails while daring greatly, so that his place shall never be with those cold and timid souls who know neither victory nor defeat." Setbacks - many people equate them with "failure". Setbacks do not mean you failed, they simply mean you tried. This is the victory - the victory is trying. As Roosevelt said, "if he fails, he fails while daring greatly" If you let them, your setbacks will teach you things success never could.

I am not talking about the kind of failure you slap a motivational quote over and post on Instagram to get view and likes. I am talking about the kind of failure that hits like a punch to the ribs, the kind that shows up uninvited, unrelenting, and unmoved by how well you planned and that leaves you sitting in your truck at the end of the day, staring through the windshield, asking yourself, "What the hell just happened?" That kind of setback stings and messes with your confidence. It challenges your sense of direction and depending on the day or week you have had; it might even make you want to give up. However, if you lean into it—not run from it—it can become the most valuable thing that ever happened to you, because the truth of the matter is: a setback is not the end, it is a signal - life's way of saying, "Something is not aligned here. Let us take another look."

Setbacks Are Course-Correctors

Sometimes setbacks come out of nowhere, while other times, we saw them coming but did not want to believe the signs. Either way, when they show up, they have a way of making us pause and force us to take a hard look at our priorities, our habits, our assumptions—and sometimes, if we are honest, even our identity. I have had setbacks that made me question everything. Career moves I thought were surefire, relationships I was sure would last, moments where I thought I had everything dialed in, only to realize I was standing on sand, not rock. As painful as those moments were, I can tell you this without hesitation: the best lessons I have ever learned did not come from my wins, they came from the stumbles. The key to this is to not just move on because you must also learn from the setback, so you do not go down that path again. Learn.

When something does not work out, you have two choices, you can shove it in a box, pretend it never happened, and keep walking in the same direction, or you can ask the tougher questions: What went wrong here? What was I assuming? What part of this did I control—and what didn't I? What would I do differently next time?

This is not about assigning blame, it is about gaining insight and seeing where things went wrong. It is about seeing with clarity, and it is about maturity. Sometimes what you learn from a setback becomes the very foundation of your next breakthrough. I have watched people rebuild after a failed business and find their calling in something they never would have considered before. I have seen relationships fall apart and make room for deeper healing and wholeness and I have known officers who lost promotions or made mistakes on duty, only to become the most grounded leaders I have ever served with. That is not failure. That is redirection.

Resilience Is Not Just Getting Back Up—It is Getting Back Up Wiser

There is a difference between bouncing back and growing forward. Resilience is not just toughness, as many people doing memes on Instagram think it is. It is adaptability, it is the willingness to stay in the game when you have bruises, and it is standing back up after a hit and saying: "Okay, that did not work. Now what?" Resilience is not pretending the hit did not hurt, it is choosing not to stay down because of it. I have watched strong men cry in patrol cars, squad rooms, and kitchens and I have seen confident people second-guess everything they believed about themselves after a divorce, a layoff, a diagnosis. I have done it myself—more than once and here is what I know from these experiences: that moment of doubt? It does not disqualify you, it reveals you and shows you where you have been relying on pride instead of principle. It shows you where your foundation needs reinforcement and where your character is still being forged. If you stay with it—if you let it teach you, you will come out of it better, clearer, and stronger.

Rethinking the Word "Failure"

This is one of the worst and most wrongly used words in the English language. I hate it. We toss around the word "failure" like it is a final judgment, but most of the time, it is not failure at all. It is an education, feedback, and refinement. You did not fail because the job did not work out or because you poured your heart into something, and it did not go the way you hoped or because the thing you built fell apart. If you do not stay down and you get back up, assess and try again, then you failed forward and that counts. Here is the irony: the people who judge you for it? They are usually the ones too scared to try anything themselves and you have seen it too. It is the people on IG or Facebook or TikTok talking negatively about people and their passions, but when you look at their page, they have nothing to show for their lives. They do not have the guts to take a risk and put their money where their mouths are - so keep going.

What looks like failure from the outside might be the exact fire you needed to burn away what was not serving you. Several factors may warrant consideration: at times, a business may fail because its objectives were not aligned with your personal aspirations. Occasionally, opportunities end as they may no longer suit your evolving identity. Likewise, setbacks can occur when growth in skills or character has not yet matched the pace of ambition. Remember from Chapter 6, failure is not the enemy. Ego is, because ego says: "You must get it right the first time. Mistakes make you weak. You should have known better. You should have done better." But growth says: "You tried. You learned. You are wiser now. Keep going." That is not weakness. That is wisdom.

The Cost of Playing It Safe

I will be blunt here; the fear of failure keeps more people stuck than failure itself ever will. We would rather stay comfortable in a job that is draining us, or a relationship that is going nowhere, than risk the sting of trying and failing - BUT - there is a cost to that comfort, and it is called regret. Regret does not show up loud, it shows up slowly and quietly like rust on metal. It creeps into your thoughts in the middle of the night and whispers: "What if you had gone for it?" or "What if you had tried?" Personally, I'd rather live with a scar than with that question because a scar means you were in the fight and means you showed up and risked something. Sometimes that risk does not pay off right away, but it changes you, deepens you, and prepares you for the next thing.

The only thing worse than failing is never stepping into the arena at all. There is a quote my friend Rand Padgett read to me one time and I think it is one of the most powerful statements I have ever heard about what we are talking about here. It is from a British Cleric/Pastor Sydney Smith and goes as follows, "Regret for the things we did can be tempered by time; it is regret for the things we did not do that is inconsolable." Remember, just because we make a mistake does not mean it will haunt us forever, but do you want to be on your death bed regretting all the things you did not try? Do the thing!

Start Again—Not from Scratch, But from Experience

Setbacks strip away illusion and they get rid of the fluff while exposing the parts of us we thought were strong but were not. When the dust settles, you get to start again - but you are not starting from zero, you are starting from experience and that is your edge. That is the gold lining of the cloud, because you know what works now and you know what does not. You know how it felt to ignore your gut—and what happened when you did, you know how to spot red flags, and you know how to trust your instincts. You have been tested and now you get to build with intention, lead from wisdom, love with boundaries, dream with discipline, trust more carefully—but also more fully. You are not just older, you are seasoned and that is a substantial difference.

Let the Setback Refine You—Not Define You

This part's important- You can carry the lesson without carrying the shame. Stop beating yourself up about setbacks, let that setback be a teacher, not a prison. Do not let it build walls around your heart and do not let it close you off from people, from purpose, from progress, because you are much more than the deal that fell through, than the uniform you no longer wear, the marriage that ended, the dream that died, or the job that let you go. You are not your lowest moment, and you are still in the fight, so stand back up and brush off the dust, then ask better questions and walk with deeper wisdom, because you are not broken. You are being rebuilt and that rebuilding process? That painful, honest, grinding process? Well, that is where real transformation happens and where you find strength you did not know you had, clarity, you did not know you needed, and a voice you did not know was buried inside you.

The Quiet Strength of Showing Up Again

You do not have to shout your comeback - stay off social media. Just live it because you do not have to prove your worth to anyone. Getting back up after a setback is often quiet work because it is the work no one sees and it is done in early mornings and late nights, in therapy sessions and prayer closets, in silent car rides and sweaty gym floors. It is done when you choose not to give up on yourself and you do not need applause because what you really need now is alignment with who you are now, with what you have learned, and with where you are going.

Real World Example: Kevin McCurdy – McCurdy Wood and Metal

I would like you to meet my friend Kevin, who exemplifies everything we talked about in this chapter. Kevin didn't plan to leave the job when he did, as like most of us who wear the badge, he figured he'd see it through to the finish line on his own terms. He spent years serving San Bernardino County as a sheriff's deputy, detective, and sergeant— quietly dependable, the kind of guy you wanted next to you when things went sideways, but sometimes life makes the decision for you. Due to medical issues, Kevin was forced into retirement earlier than expected and for a man built on service, that kind of pivot hits different. You don't just lose a job, you lose identity, routine, and brotherhood. One day you are performing routine duties and participating in meetings with your team, and the next you find yourself at home with no specific tasks to complete. That kind of transition breaks some people, but not Kevin.

He leaned into something else that had been sitting quietly in the background: his ability to build. What started as a way to pass time and make extra money during his time as a LEO, quickly turned into a way to continue his life without the badge. He continued crafting furniture, welding, shaping, and designing, and while there was no uniform, no badge, no gun and no radio on his hip, there was purpose. That's how McCurdy Wood & Metal was born. It didn't come with a business plan or a big announcement, it came with renting a building, moving in and then taking on one project at a time, as Kevin slowly redirected the same discipline and precision he used in law enforcement toward his craft. Working with wood and steel gave him a new way to serve—not in a patrol car, but with a welder, a saw, and a vision.

And here's the thing: when the world sees a man medically retired, they often assume he's broken or done, but Kevin is living proof that a chapter ending doesn't mean the story's over, because he is not just surviving post-career—he's building something lasting and beautiful and he brings the same grit to his workshop that he brought to every shift: attention to detail, a refusal to cut corners, and the kind of quiet pride that comes from doing things the right way even when nobody's watching. His pieces aren't just furniture; they're testimony and proof that you can still build a life of meaning even after the lights go out and the uniform is folded for the last time.

Today, McCurdy Wood & Metal is growing, and so is Kevin. He's found a way to transform pain into purpose; to shape loss into legacy and he's done it with humility, resilience, and the kind of strength that doesn't make noise, it just gets to work. That's the pivot. It is not always chosen, but accepted and it is never easy, but honorable. Kevin didn't want to leave the job—but he refused to let the job leaving him be the end of the road.

Final Thoughts: Faithful Over Flawless

Please take this point with you - you do not have to be flawless. It is essential to remain committed—to the process, the lessons learned, ongoing personal development, and above all, to maintaining integrity with oneself. Your story is not over because you hit a wall. It is evolving and what looks like an end today might be the very thing that launches your next chapter, so when the setback comes—and it will—do not panic, pause. Listen. Learn. Then step forward, not with fear, but with faith because if you let it, that setback will do more for your future than success ever could.

📓 Reflection & Action

1. What part of this chapter resonated with you most? Why?
2. What is one action you can take this week to apply a principle discussed here?
3. Are there any habits or beliefs you need to let go of to pivot successfully?
4. Who can you talk to for support or accountability around this pivot?

14

14. Mental and Physical Well-being — Your Foundation in the Pivot

Your well-being—mental and physical—is the foundation that holds everything together when life throws that curve-ball. I have seen a lot of people pushed to their breaking point—out in the field, in family rooms, behind desks—and the ones who came through were not the toughest or the loudest, they were the ones who took care of themselves when everything felt like it was falling apart. Not in flashy ways and certainly not with Instagram wellness quotes or green smoothies. They took care of themselves quietly, intelligently and deliberately and because of that, they endured.

Trust me, this is not about perfection or being "jacked," it is about grit, resilience, and a dedication to yourself. Without your health - your mind steady and your body able, you will not have the fuel to make it through your pivot, much less build something meaningful on the other side. So, let's talk about it—not as a luxury, but as a mission-critical priority.

Why Your Mental and Physical Health Matters

In law enforcement, I learned early on: when your head and body are off, the whole operation suffers, and it is the same when you are going through any major life change. Yet, this is often the very thing we ignore because we get so caught up on what is next, what needs to be done, who needs us, what is uncertain, and that we push ourselves to the back of the line. If you are going to stand strong through transition, you must put your well-being front and center.

Mental Health

Resilience - it's a trendy word, but it is proper - as it is the core of staying in the fight. Life is going to test you with setbacks, doubts, and curve-balls—they are guaranteed. Resilience does not mean those tests do not hurt, it means you do not stay down. It means you get up, learn something, and move forward anyway. That muscle? Yes, the one between your ears. That one is built daily through how you treat your mind. Focus on these things:

- Clarity - When you are in the middle of a transition, the world gets loud. Your mind races, anxiety creeps in and you start questioning everything. Mental clarity is your lifeline in that storm because you do not need all the answers, you just need to see the next step clearly and that is enough to get you moving.
- Emotional Balance - Pivoting is not just a tactical change, it is an emotional roller-coaster, where you will feel excitement, grief, guilt, fear, joy—sometimes all in one day. Mental health does not mean never feeling those things, it means feeling them without letting them drive the car off the road. It is the difference between reacting and responding.

Physical Health

- Energy - You can have all the vision and passion in the world, but if your tank is empty, it does not matter because fatigue will rob you of your momentum. You need fuel in the form of rest, healthy food, and movement to keep driving forward.
- Immune Function - Stress beats your body down. Hard. When you are constantly in fight-or-flight mode, your body never gets to heal, which opens the door to sickness—and that knocks you off the pivot path fast. Staying physically healthy means you are less likely to be sidelined when life demands your best.
- Overall, Balance - Your body and your mind are constantly talking to each other and if you neglect one, the other suffers. Keep both tuned, and suddenly you can think clearer, move better, and manage more without crumbling.

Managing Stress: Real-World Tools That Work

Stress is not optional in a pivot, but suffering? That is optional. You do not have to be a therapist or yogi to use tools that keep you steady, you just must start with what is real. Mindfulness - strip the fluff from this word, Mindfulness just means presence. Awareness - spend five minutes noticing your breath, sitting on your porch and just listening, or taking a walk without your phone. Awareness interrupts the mental chaos and brings you back to now, and now is where change happens. Meditation - this is not a mysterious, mystical thing and there is no need for incense or a guru. You just need to be still and breathe. Relax and let your thoughts come and go like cars passing on a street. It is a simple act to allow you to briefly get off the merry go round for a minute, because even five minutes a day can change your brain—and your nervous system.

Breathing Exercises - I use this every night and when stressed - try this right now: Breathe in for 4 seconds. Hold for 7. Breathe out for 8. Do that three or four times. That 4-7-8 pattern tells your body you are safe and that it is okay to stop panicking. It is a tool I have used in high-pressure moments and works.

Progressive Muscle Relaxation - Start at your toes and clench them for a few seconds. Then release. Move up through your body—legs, hips, chest, arms, face. This reminds your body that it does not have to be on high alert all the time and gives you your calm back.

Movement, Food, and Sleep: The Essentials

Look, I am not here to sell you on fitness challenges or super foods, as I have no idea about all that. What I am here to tell you that the small, basic stuff? It matters.

Keep Moving - Movement is medicine and it clears your mind, boosts your mood, and helps you process emotions stuck in your body. You do not need a gym, you just need consistency, so walk the neighborhood, stretch before bed, or do push-ups in the morning. Whatever you do, move.

Eat to Fuel - I will start with this caveat- I am not a nutritionist, nor do I play one on TV. This just seems to be common sense information picked up over a lifetime of working with and watching how fit people eat versus how unfit people eat. Food is more than comfort. It is your body's fuel and the better the fuel, the better you will perform, so start small: Cut the soda. Eat more real food—things that grow, not things in a wrapper. Drink more water than you think you need. You will notice the difference in your brain, your focus, and your mood.

Protect Your Sleep - Sleep is where healing happens, and it is when your body repairs itself and your mind processes the day. If you sleep four hours a night, running on caffeine and adrenaline, you are not pivoting, you are surviving, and that is a recipe for burnout. Create a nighttime routine and shut the screens down early and go to bed like your life depends on it—because in a way, it does.

Recognizing and Fighting Burnout

Burnout is not about being tired, it is about being empty - it is a soul-level drain that no nap can fix, so make sure you are looking for signs of burnout: you are numb—nothing excites you anymore, you feel overwhelmed all the time, you are constantly irritable or checked out, or you have lost interest in what used to matter. If any of these sounds familiar, do not ignore it, as it could be a big red flag of things coming down the road. So, how do we prevent burnout? Here are a few ideas: set boundaries, say no, protect your time, take real breaks, step away from your phone and go outside, say no without guilt, and schedule for Joy. Do not wait for joy to happen, you must make time for it. It does not matter what it is: a hobby or music or anything that lights you up.

Recovering from Burnout? Talk to Someone, do not isolate, find someone who will listen without fixing, and rest intentionally. Stop multitasking - no "I'll just check email while I lie down." Get real rest and then reevaluate your goals: are they still yours, or are you chasing something that does not fit you anymore?

Prioritize Yourself When Everything Feels Unsteady

During your pivot - or really any time - life tilts and you feel like you are losing your grip, remember: You are your anchor - not your job, not your relationship, and not your bank account. You and only you. So, here is what that looks like: Make self-care non-negotiable - put it on the calendar like a meeting, practice presence - even if it is 30 seconds of breath, it matters, stay connected - text a friend to for coffee because connection steadies the soul, and finally, be gentle with yourself - change is hard, but you are doing it and THAT is what counts.

Final Thoughts: Your Well-being Is Your Mission

Let us be real—this path you are on? It is not the easy one, and you could have stayed in the old thing and let fear win, but you did not do that. You are choosing to pivot, to grow, and to transform. Make no mistake, that choice is going to test you in ways you have not considered. Your mind will waver and your body will ache and the doubt will whisper.

That is why taking care of your well-being is not optional, it is essential and is what lets you keep walking when the trail gets rough, so eat, move, rest, reflect, laugh, and connect. Do the little things, because those little things add up to strength and that strength is what will carry you through the storm—and into the life you are building on the other side.

📓 Reflection & Action

1. What part of this chapter resonated with you most? Why?
2. What is one action you can take this week to apply a principle discussed here?
3. Are there any habits or beliefs you need to let go of to pivot successfully?
4. Who can you talk to for support or accountability around this pivot?

V

Part Five

Movement and Momentum

15

15. Get Off the X — Moving When It Matters Most

There is a phrase used in tactical and military circles that carries a heavy weight — one that can mean the difference between life and death. That phrase is "Get off the X." In combat, "the X" is the kill zone — the spot where a unit has been ambushed, caught off guard, or trapped in a deadly crossfire and it is the place where every second counts, where hesitation is lethal. The principle is simple: if you stay on the X, you die and if you move — even if you do not know where you are going — you increase your chances of survival. Getting off the X is about immediate action; it is about getting out of danger first and figuring out the rest later. Now, this might sound like a lesson reserved for the battlefield, but here is the truth — we all find ourselves on the X at some point in life and while it may not be a firefight with guns blazing, sometimes it is subtler but just as dangerous: a toxic job, a broken relationship, crushing debt, an identity crisis, or a moment when the walls come crashing down and nothing feels stable anymore. No matter the shape or size of the X, the truth remains the same: the longer you stay in that pressure zone—emotionally, mentally, or physically, the harder it becomes to move, and the more damage it causes.

Recognizing You Are on the X

The hardest part about getting off the X is often not the movement itself — it is recognizing that you are on it in the first place, because life has a sneaky way of normalizing dysfunction. We tell ourselves things like: "It's just a rough patch," "I'm used to this," or "It could be worse." But deep inside, your body and soul are signaling a different truth - you may have a pit in your stomach you cannot shake, a stillness or heaviness in your chest, or a whisper in your mind that says, "You're not okay here." Those signals are not just mood swings or stress; they are flares in the night sky—your internal warning system screaming: "This is the X." Think critically about it - are you waking up every day with a sense of dread? Do you find yourself numbing out just to get through the day? Are you compromising your values to keep the peace or avoid conflict? Do you feel stuck but terrified of change? If the answer is yes to any of these, you are likely standing right on that danger zone.

Why People Freeze

The human brain and body are wired for survival, but not always in the way we want when we face life's hardest moments. You have all heard of the fight, flight, or freeze reaction. Many times, if you are not trained for it, when overwhelmed, our natural response is often to freeze. This is a biological response inherited from our ancestors — when faced with a threat too big to fight or flee from, freezing could keep you unnoticed, buying precious seconds to assess or avoid harm. But we are not hiding from a saber tooth tiger anymore, and in life, that freeze often looks like: procrastination, denial, distraction, or disconnection and we tell ourselves, "I need more time," "I'll figure it out later," "I just need a little more money," or "When things settle down, I'll make a move."

We wait for the perfect plan, or the perfect timing, or for a rescuer to show up, but there is no perfect plan, or perfect timing, and seldom is there a knight in shining armor coming. In a real ambush, time is your enemy and in life, it is no different. The longer you stay frozen on the X, the more it drains you, the fear sinks deeper roots, your options narrow, and your momentum dies. You are not broken for freezing, but you are at risk of getting stuck.

Moving Does Not Require a Map

Here is the thing you need to know — you do not need a perfect map to get moving. You do not need all the answers, you just need to take the first step because movement is not about perfection, it is about motion. It might be messy, and it might feel awkward, but moving creates space - to breathe, to think, and to build. A first move may look like this - take a deep breath and make the call you have been avoiding, say the truth you have been holding inside, quit the job that is draining your soul, ask for help - even if it is scary, file that paper work, or try something that terrifies you. If you just take the first step — however uncertain — it chips away at the hold the X has on you - and it gives you a burst of dopamine, which feels good and can help you want to take the next step.

Get Off the X in Your Life

Now, let us bring it home. What is your X? And what would getting off it look like? If your X is burnout, maybe it starts with asking for time off. If it is a toxic relationship, maybe it is speaking your truth or setting a boundary. If it is a fiscal crisis, maybe it is downsizing or getting brutally honest about your numbers. If it is shame, maybe it is finally telling your story. Whatever your X looks like, here is the most important part: do not wait for everything to be tidy, do not wait for certainty, just take the first faithful step in a direction that feels like freedom, even if the path is not clear.

Movement Is Survival and Reclamation

Getting off the X is survival, yes — but it is more than that, it is about reclaiming your agency and refusing to let life's worst moments pin you down. It is about choosing motion over stagnation, courage over comfort, and purpose over paralysis. You were not built to die on the X, you were built to move, to pivot, and to rise. Movement does not always look heroic or grand, sometimes it is quiet and messy. I have seen folks start with small, barely noticeable changes that transformed their lives, like a mother overwhelmed by the chaos of single parenting begins saying "no" to extra commitments so she can breathe, a man stuck in a dead-end job picks up a night class to learn a new skill, or a woman trapped in toxic friendships starts accepting invitations from new people who challenge her to grow. Those first moves might seem tiny, but they add up because every inch you put between yourself, and the X is a win.

Overcoming Fear and Doubt

Fear and doubt are natural and when you are pinned on the X, they are louder than ever, but remember this: fear is not the enemy, it is a compass pointing to where courage is needed and doubt does not mean you are failing, it means you are human. When the enemy on the battlefield closes in, soldiers do not wait for perfect clarity—they move forward with what they have and the same principle applies to you.

Tools to Help You Get Moving

Tools, strategies, or support from others may be required in certain situations. Here are some options to consider:

1. Break It Down - Big pivots are overwhelming, so break your move into small, actionable steps. For example, if you want to leave a toxic job, your first step might be updating your resume - not quitting that day but starting the process.
2. Build Accountability - Tell a trusted friend or mentor about your plan and ask them to check in, because accountability creates momentum.
3. Practice Self-Compassion - Movement does not mean you will not stumble, it means you keep getting up and you do not beat yourself up for fears or setbacks. You should be your own strongest supporter.

A Word on Waiting

Sometimes, you might think waiting is safer, but waiting without movement is a trap. Waiting for the perfect time, the perfect plan, or the perfect mood often becomes a way to stay stuck and movement does not mean rushing blindly, it means starting and then adjusting as you go. Remember this, no plan survives first contact with reality, but movement gives you the time, space, and chance to adapt. The moment you get off the X is the moment you step into possibility, and it can be scary, uncertain, and uncomfortable - but it is also where life begins again. If you are reading this and feeling stuck, I want you to know that you are not alone. You are not weak or broken - you are human and you were built for motion, so get up, move, and keep moving. The path forward will not always be clear, but the one thing I guarantee is that movement creates hope and hope is the spark that fuels every pivot worth making.

Look Up and Out — Breaking the Cycle of Survival Thinking

When you are in survival mode — when life hits hard and you are just trying to stay afloat, your focus narrows and you stop thinking long-term. You stop imagining possibilities and your world becomes small, so you take just the next step, the next breath, the next moment and that kind of focus can save your life in a crisis. But if you stay there too long, it can also steal your future and that is why, once you have gotten off the X — once you have made the initial move out of danger — the next vital pivot is this: you must look up and out. You must lift your head and expand your vision. You must remember that you were made not just to survive, but to live.

What Happens When You Look Down Too Long

When you stay head-down too long, you start to internalize the struggle and stop believing there is anything better waiting for you. You think the pain defines you and that narrow view becomes your only view and you have seen it in people who stay in bad situations not because they must, but because they have forgotten how to want more and you have seen it in folks who stop dreaming, who stop taking risks, and who trade hope for habit. It is like driving through a storm with your eyes glued to the dashboard — you are moving, but you are not really seeing and if you cannot see where you are going, you are likely to end up somewhere you never meant to be.

Look Up: Reclaim Your Sense of Direction - looking up means reclaiming a sense of vision and remembering that your life has more chapters ahead, and that you still get a say in how they unfold. It can be as simple as asking yourself where you want to be six months from now, or thinking about what used to make you feel alive before things got heavy, or even what would you chase if fear did not have a vote? When you look up, you shift from reaction to intention and you start noticing things you missed when your head was down — opportunities, relationships, open doors. This is how you reconnect to hope and how you steer, not just stumble.

Look Out: Reconnect to the Bigger World - looking out means re-membering you are not alone in your story. It is about connection, contribution, and compassion. When we isolate ourselves in hardship, the world feels cold and tight, but when we reach back out — even in small ways — it stretches us and heals something within us. Looking out takes the shape of volunteering your time or story, listening to someone else's journey, or asking how you can serve, not just how you can survive. And sometimes, looking out just means stepping outside and noticing the world has not stopped turning — the sky is still big, the sun still rises, people still laugh, dream, build, and heal. That matters more than it seems.

The Day I Finally Looked Up

There was a time after I stepped away from the badge when I still had not fully embraced the pivot. I had gotten off the X — retired, survived — but I was walking through life like I was still under fire with my head down, shoulders tight, and a lack of vision. I was at the shop one afternoon sanding a piece of light fixture, and I caught myself just... standing there. Frozen. Not working. Not thinking. Just existing. Then I heard my granddaughter outside laughing. Real laughter — that full-belly, no-worry kind. I stepped outside and saw her hitting tennis balls with my wife, with not a care in the world, and it hit me, I had not looked up in months. I had let the new normal take over the old normal and it broke something loose in me. Not all at once — but enough to realize I was still living like the old life had not ended. It was enough to ask myself: what am I missing by staying small? That was the beginning of me dreaming again, thinking of authoring this book that I had put off repeatedly— building again — living with my head up.

How to Start Looking Up and Out

So, if you have been in the trenches for a while, lifting your gaze might feel unnatural, so start small. The following are some suggestions: Create space for reflection. Quiet mornings. A journal. A walk without your phone. Feed your imagination. Read a book that has nothing to do with survival. Watch someone else's comeback story. Talk to people who dream. Get around folks who are building, not just coping. Celebrate tiny victories. When you look up even a little, mark it. That is movement. And if you catch yourself slipping back into head-down thinking — be gentle. Just return to the habit. Repeatedly, look up. Look out.

Real World Example: Brett Waterman - TV Host and Restoration Specialist

Life, leadership, pivoting is about relationship building and maintaining relationships and one of the oldest relationships I have is with Brett. I've known Brett Waterman for as long as I can remember. Our parents were friends before I was born, so Brett was always a fixture in my life— like an older brother who carved his own path but never lost touch with where he came from. Brett's gift—the ability to see not just what is, but what could be—has defined his life's work.

Before Brett became the host of Restored, he took a path that, on the surface, looked nothing like what he does now. After earning dual degrees in Political Science and History from UCLA, he spent years working on the corporate side of Lexus and Mercedes-Benz as these luxury automotive brands were expanding in the U.S. Those early years gave him valuable skills in operations, planning, and precision— qualities that would later serve him well in preservation. But even then, his passion for craftsmanship never left him. Nights and weekends, Brett was often immersed in projects that let him work with his hands, reviving the old and giving it new life. That balance between his day job and his passion ultimately led to a pivotal moment: walking away from the corporate track to devote himself entirely to architectural preservation. This type of pivot can be scary, as you are giving up a lucrative salary and benefits in the corporate world to step out into the unknown and take on work in restoration and construction - which can be very "feast or famine." But Brett did not let that fear stop him and he pivoted anyway and let the chips fall where they may.

Through grit, determination and a lot of hard work, Brett has spent more than 30 years restoring historic homes across Southern California, always focusing on authenticity—using original techniques and materials wherever possible. When he launched Restored, it wasn't about becoming a TV personality, it was about sharing the value of doing things right—preserving history while creating something lasting. Working on the show alongside him and contributing my woodworking has been a full-circle moment for me. Even now, I continue to do woodworking for Brett, and every project feels like stepping into a story bigger than either of us as we bring the past back to life.

Brett's work on another series, Unlocking History, takes that same passion and digs deeper into the stories behind historic properties— the architects, craftsmen, and homeowners who shaped these places. What I've learned from him is that preservation is never just about wood and nails; it's about understanding the soul of a place and his dedication to the finer details, from the grain of the wood to the curve of a hand-carved trim, reminds me that true craftsmanship is as much about respect as it is about skill.

Growing up with Brett, I've seen his journey firsthand. He didn't stumble into success; he built it, one deliberate choice at a time. His pivot from the corporate world to preservation taught me something important about following your calling: sometimes the pivot isn't about finding something new, but about returning to what you've loved all along.

When I walk onto one of Brett's job sites, I don't just see construction or design—I see legacy. I see the fingerprints of the craftsmen who came before us and the care Brett takes to honor their work. Working with him, both on Restored and beyond, is more than just a professional collaboration; it's a reminder that some of the best pivots in life are about digging deeper into your roots rather than abandoning them and never being afraid to chase that which you love and are passionate about.

Brett's story is proof that when you respect the past and build with purpose, in any field, you are not just restoring a "thing", you are restoring your soul - and that is a pivot worth taking.

Final Thoughts

Getting off the X saves your life, but looking up and out? That is how you start to live again and is how you begin to build a future you want — not just one you can survive. This is not about ignoring the pain you have walked through; it is about remembering that you are still here, and you are still breathing. If you are still breathing, you are still becoming - so, take a deep breath, lift your head, and look around because there is more out there and there is more left in you.

📓 Reflection & Action

1. What part of this chapter resonated with you most? Why?
2. What is one action you can take this week to apply a principle discussed here?
3. Are there any habits or beliefs you need to let go of to pivot successfully?
4. Who can you talk to for support or accountability around this pivot?

16

16. Decide and Act — Momentum Over Perfection

At some point in every pivot, you reach a moment that changes everything and it is not the moment you realize you need to change; it is not the moment you wrestle with your doubts or face your fears; it is the moment you decide. When you choose a path, any path, and then take the first step on it. You have done the soul-searching, and you have sat in the hard conversations — sometimes with others, sometimes alone in the dark. You have looked up and out, off the X, and told the truth and you have confronted your own reflection and faced what you need to do.

Now comes the part that scares more people than anything else: you must decide - and then you must act.

There is something about decision and action that shakes people to their core, because for all the planning, hoping, and praying — nothing moves until you do. You must leave the starting line, and you must step into the unknown, and the longer you wait, the heavier that moment feels, the more fear builds and the more you convince yourself that staying put feels safer. But waiting is a lie and while waiting feels like safety, it is really a trap. It feels like control, but it is losing control and when you hover near a decision, when you run the pros and cons over and over, you might call it reflection or wise caution, but many times it is just stalling. It is telling yourself you need one more conversation, one more doctor's opinion, one more sign. "I'm just not ready yet," you say, but here is the truth: you will never be ready. You will never have 100% clarity, and the perfect moment will never come.

If you wait until you feel completely certain — emotionally, financially, mentally — you will still be in the same place a year from now, just more tired, more frustrated, and more stuck. It is like when you hear people say they are waiting until they are "financially sound" to have children... you will never get there. ACT! This is where a lot of good people get stuck — in the trap we call paralysis by analysis. I saw it all the time on the job, officers with the right training, the right mindset, and the right intentions... but when it came time to move, they froze. Not because they did not care or were not capable, but because they were trying to think their way to perfect certainty. Life does not offer that luxury, but we tell ourselves we are being responsible — "just gathering all the facts." But often, we are just afraid because we do not want to make the wrong move, so we make no move. And let me tell you, no move is often the worst one you can make.

Paralysis by analysis is what happens when your brain convinces you that more time, more information, or more discussion will protect you from failure. The reality is, the longer you wait, the more momentum you lose, and once momentum is gone, getting started again takes twice the energy. I had a friend who wanted to leave his corporate job to start his own woodworking business, so he spent two years researching, planning, watching tutorials, pricing out every tool. He could have launched twice over and eventually, I told him straight — "Brother, you do not need another spreadsheet. You need to make your first cut."

The antidote to overthinking is not more thinking. It is movement because action creates clarity, not the other way around and most people believe they need to have it all figured out before they move forward. But clarity, real clarity, is something you earn by stepping into motion and it is when you take that first step that you begin to see the path more clearly. You learn what works and what does not, what energizes you and what drains you, and what feels right and what needs to be adjusted. I have seen this truth repeatedly — in the lives of entrepreneurs launching a business, artists picking up their brushes, people rebuilding their lives after hardship. None of them thought their way into their new lives, they moved their way there one step at a time.

I know because I lived it. When I was on the cusp of leaving law enforcement, I was undecided for months. I knew deep down the time had come, because my body screamed it — the injuries, the pain, the exhaustion — I didn't say it out loud, but my mind kept circling, stuck in fear of the next step. I told myself I needed one more doctor's visit, one more conversation, one more bit of reassurance, afraid that if I made the wrong move, everything I had built would fall apart. The day I finally walked into the office and signed the paperwork, I did not feel brave or triumphant, yes there was relief, but I also felt exposed, scared, sick. But then something shifted — not peace, exactly — but movement, because I was no longer waiting, I was living.

From there, the next decisions came easier. Continuing saying yes to woodworking commissions, getting the shop ready for full time work, and speaking aloud about what I really wanted. That first step unlocked the door, and it made the rest possible. I remember talking to a friend who wanted to start his own business but was frozen by the "what ifs." What if I fail? What if I cannot provide? What if I am not good enough? But then he decided. Not a perfect one, just a decision and he ACTED. He called a mentor, opened a bank account, ordered supplies and while he did not know how it would turn out — he moved. Months later, he told me that the first step was the hardest — but it saved him. I want you to feel that same spark.

Instead of drowning in "what ifs," ask yourself, "What is the next right step I can take today? What would I do if I trusted myself for five minutes? What am I willing to risk getting unstuck?" You do not need a ten-year plan; you need to move. The people who navigate change well are not those with all the answers, but those with a bias toward action. They know small steps build confidence and that waiting builds fear. In the SWAT world, and in many special forces units, that is how you train - crawl, walk, run. You start out small and build on the small successes. You do not need to move fast or perfectly — you just need to move with intention and while you might not know exactly where you will end up, that is okay — pick a direction that feels honest, healthy, and hopeful and begin there. It is important to recognize that making a decision does not constitute a lifelong commitment; there is always the opportunity to make adjustments and re-calibrate as necessary. However, progress cannot be achieved without taking initial action, because movement invites learning.

If you know what you need to do, do not let more than a day pass without acting. Make the call, set the meeting, cancel the thing, and start the thing. Time is the enemy of momentum, and remember, confidence is not something you wait for, it is something you build. It is the byproduct of action, not a prerequisite and you do not need to feel brave first — just be brave enough to act long enough. Momentum matters more than perfection and I have learned this lesson many times on the street and in life. Hesitation can cost lives and when doubt creeps in, the enemy closes in. A well-timed, imperfect move can open space, create opportunity, and shift the entire battle, while waiting for perfection is like standing still in quicksand, the harder you try to fight it, the faster you sink. Momentum pulls you out.

While you may be afraid that action will cost you, remember that inaction carries a cost too, though it is easy to overlook. Inaction results in lost opportunities, strained relationships, health suffering under stress, dreams deferred until they feel impossible — all these pile up and that cost compounds like interest on a loan. One year of hesitation can become five years of regret. Deciding and acting in real life is messy and unpredictable and it might mean quitting a job before the next one is lined up, leaving a relationship that no longer serves you, starting therapy even though you are terrified, moving to a new city with nothing but a suitcase and hope, or saying no to something you once said yes to. Substantial changes are built from countless small decisions and every decision builds momentum.

Leaping into the unknown feels like free fall, but here is how you steady yourself: plan for the worst and hope for the best. Know what you will do if things do not go as planned and build safety nets. Find people you trust to hold you accountable and practice small acts of courage daily — saying no when you want to say yes, speaking your truth in small ways. Re-frame fear as excitement; physiologically, they feel the same, so they choose to see adrenaline as fuel, not poison.

For many of us, faith is the backbone of courage, and it is what lets us trust that even when we cannot see the full path, something bigger is guiding us. Faith is not sitting back doing nothing. Faith is getting up and moving forward, even when the road ahead is foggy. It is deciding and then trusting momentum will carry you. Perfectionism is a silent killer of pivots because it convinces you to delay, polish endlessly, prepare forever. It whispers that your idea is not good enough, your timing is not right, your confidence is not real. If perfection were a person, I would tell it to take a long walk off a short pier.

In practice, meaningful change is achieved through decisive action rather than hesitation or over-analysis. Progress occurs when you make decisions and take initiative, not by waiting until every detail is resolved and it occurs when you stop dancing around the edge and leap — even if your hands shake and your voice cracks. So, here is your invitation: stop circling the runway, stop gathering endless opinions, stop waiting for a sign.

Make the decision. Take the step. Trust that motion will create the momentum you need. Because the life you want? It is waiting on the other side of action.

📓 Reflection & Action

1. What part of this chapter resonated with you most? Why?
2. What is one action you can take this week to apply a principle discussed here?
3. Are there any habits or beliefs you need to let go of to pivot successfully?
4. Who can you talk to for support or accountability around this pivot?

VI

Part Six

Anchored in Meaning

17

17. Faith as a Compass: Trusting Something Greater in the Pivot

There is a moment at the edge of any real change—when the floor gives out, the air gets thin, and every instinct tells you to grip tighter to what you have always known. It is in that moment where faith steps in—not always loud, not always churchy, and not always organized—but real. Tangible. Steadying.

In my years in law enforcement, I have seen people on their worst days and their best and I have also faced my own demons—moments where the badge, the job, the routine that once defined me no longer held the same shape. I had to figure out what came next, and through it all, faith—mine and others'—showed up in surprising ways. Whether you are religious or not, this chapter is not about dogma, it is about something deeper: the idea that in the middle of uncertainty, there's value in trusting a force greater than yourself. For me, it is God. For you, it may be God, it might be the universe, it might be purpose, legacy, love, or service. But faith—real faith—is not passive. It is a decision to keep moving when you cannot see the whole road.

When Control Is Not an Option

Law enforcement taught me a lot about control. We trained to manage chaos, to prepare for worst-case scenarios, to stay calm when everything else was going sideways, but it also taught me the limits of control. You cannot control whether a suspect runs, you cannot control whether someone chooses sobriety, and you cannot control the economy, a diagnosis, or a sudden phone call in the middle of the night. And that lack of control? It will either break you—or it will break you open.

One of the the calls that will always stay in my soul was a baby not breathing call and mind you, this was 15 years into my career, and I thought I had seen it all. As I pulled up on scene, the street out in front of a run down apartment complex, a couple in their 20's walked up to me holding out an infant in diapers. Neither of them was crying or hysterical, which seemed odd. The mother held out her arms to me and I recognized the small, lifeless form in her hands as a baby. I took the baby from her, and she was clearly deceased with postmortem lividity clear on the back. The baby had nothing on but a diaper in the chilly morning air, and there was bruising everywhere. I knew this was more than a simple "baby not breathing" call. I asked the couple what had happened and all they would say was "She wasn't breathing when we went to get her up." Based on the condition of the little girl, that was clearly a lie as there were bruises all over her body in various stages of healing and there was clearly a history of abuse of the child. As fire arrived and took the child from me, we started the investigation. While my partners waited for the homicide detectives to arrive, I transported the male half of the couple back to the station and he did not once ask how the baby was. He sat at the station for hours and had the most nonchalant facial expression I may have ever seen - and still never asked for a status of the baby. Homicide arrived and interviewed him and after hours of lies, he finally admitted that he had gotten tired of the crying, so he stuffed the baby under a couch cushion and slept on it all night. After all my time in law enforcement, I though I had seen evil, but I was wrong – but I saw it on that day and it has never left me.

When I got back in my car, I sat and prayed. Not because I had answers, but because I did not, because I could not carry it all alone anymore. Even after growing up in church and a Christian household, that was one of the first times I realized faith was not about having certainty, it was about having somewhere to go when certainty was gone. Thank God for my wife that night. That call has had a lasting impact on me over the years and has always been right below the surface, but with determination and the assistance of a strong support system, I was able to overcome its challenges – usually.

Faith Is not a Straight Line

One of the hardest parts of the job was telling people their loved ones weren't coming home and I have seen tough guys drop to their knees when they realize their kid is not coming home, but I have also seen women in the darkest moments of grief find peace that did not make any kind of logical sense. I have also seen people curse the sky, walk away from God, lose their grip on belief entirely and if I am being honest, I have done both myself. Faith does not look the same for everyone, and it does not always look like what you would expect. Some find it in church, others in AA meetings, early morning fishing, long runs, desert meditation, or listening to hymns in their truck. It shows up in quiet decisions like forgiving someone, choosing to hope again, and showing up to put in the work.

If you are in the middle of a pivot right now, let me say this: it is okay if your faith feels shaken. It is okay if you are rebuilding it, because if I know one thing, it is that God can manage your doubt. The truth can handle your questions, so start where you are.

Faith in the Midst of Doubt

Let me tell you something that rarely gets said out loud—especially among the strong, the disciplined, the ones who are supposed to have it all figured out: even the faithful doubt. That might not sound like something you'd hear in church or from a pulpit, but I'm telling you right now, doubt is not the opposite of faith, it is part of the journey. It's the wrestling, the ache, the quiet questions you whisper when no one's around, and it is what happens when the world you trusted falls apart and you're left holding the pieces, asking, "Where was God in all of this?" I have been there and stood at the intersection of pain and silence, wondering if my prayers were bouncing off the ceiling. I have sat in my truck after a funeral, after a critical incident, after another senseless loss, and asked, "How can this be part of any divine plan?" And I've carried that confusion into retirement, into injury, into the quiet after the job ended—when the calls stopped, and the purpose I used to feel every day evaporated.

What nobody really tells you is that when the mission ends, sometimes the faith you leaned on feels like it's missing too. Not gone, not dead, but just... distant, and that distance can feel like failure - especially if you were raised to believe that doubt equals weakness, or that real faith means never questioning God. Let me offer a different truth: doubt is not failure, it is an invitation. It is a crack in the armor where the light gets in, it is the tension that stretches your understanding and forces your roots to grow deeper, and when you no longer feel the emotional high of belief, that's when real faith takes over—not the feelings, not

168

the words, but the quiet choice to keep going anyway.

The Faith That Grows in Silence

Some of the strongest believers I know have walked through long stretches of silence from God, and not because they turned their back on Him—but because they were learning to listen in new ways. Faith in those seasons isn't loud - it is not music and miracles and answered prayers, it is making the bed anyway. Showing up anyway. Loving your family anyway. Taking the next step anyway. And if you're reading this thinking, "I used to believe, but I'm not sure anymore," I want you to know this: you're not broken and you haven't lost your way, you're in the wilderness, and the wilderness is sacred ground. Scripture is full of it—men and women who loved God and still questioned Him. David. Elijah. Job. Even Christ Himself cried out from the cross, "My God, my God, why have you forsaken me?" If the Son of God can ask that question, so can you.

Rebuilding After Religion

Now some of you might not identify with traditional religion at all— and I get that. Maybe church burned you, maybe organized faith let you down, or maybe people who claimed to speak for God did more harm than good. If that's your story, I want to offer you something simple: don't let broken people define a holy God because faith isn't about pretending, it is about being honest, and sometimes honesty sounds like: "God, I'm angry," "God, I don't trust you right now," or even "God, if you're real, I need you to show up." You don't have to be cleaned up to come to God, and you don't need flowery words or polished prayers, you just need a willing heart and the guts to speak your truth.

Building Back Brick by Brick

For me, faith has become less about certainty and more about trust. Less about performance and more about presence. These days, it's not about how often I show up in a pew, it is about whether I'm showing up for the people in my life with love, humility, and grace. When I cannot feel anything spiritually, I don't panic anymore, I remember that the roots grow deepest in winter. That sometimes silence is not abandonment—it's preparation. Faith isn't about what I feel in the moment, it is about what I choose in the absence of feeling.

So if you're doubting right now? Welcome to the brotherhood. You're not disqualified. You're in good company, and the fact that you're still searching, still asking, still willing to flip these pages? That tells me everything I need to know: your faith isn't gone, it's growing quietly in the dark, and it's going to carry you further than you think.

The Role of Faith in Decision-Making

When you are pivoting—changing careers, leaving a marriage, retiring, moving across the country—logic will only get you so far. You can make a list of pros and cons, run the numbers, ask ten people for advice, but there will always be a point where the next step requires trust and that is where faith becomes practical. I do not mean blind leaps or reckless gambles, I mean a steady willingness to trust that you are not alone— that your past has prepared you, and that something greater is guiding you toward where you are supposed to be next.

Faith Grounds Your Values

The world changes fast—technology, politics, the economy, even public perception of who we are as law enforcement officers, and in all that noise, faith helps us stay rooted. It reminds us of who we are when the badge comes off and it reminds us to be kind when it is easier to be bitter. It reminds us to serve, even when no one is watching, because faith does not make life easier, it makes it clearer. It gives you a compass when the map gets torn up and reminds you that the work you are doing— even if it is new, even if it is messy, is still sacred. I once heard a pastor say, "God wastes nothing." It took a long time, but I believe that. All the trauma, all the confusion, and all the years that feel lost all build something in you that gets used later. Faith takes all the fragments and says, "Watch what I can do with this."

Letting Go of the Outcome

This is one of the hardest things to do during a pivot: surrender the outcome. We want guarantees and we want to know if the new job will be better, the relationship will last, the next season will be smoother than the last. But here is the truth I have learned—both in uniform and out of it: faith asks us to act in obedience, not control. That means doing the next right thing, even if the result is not guaranteed, it means applying for that school or certification, making that phone call, going to that therapist, starting that business—not because you know it will work, but because it feels aligned with who you are called to be.

When I first started woodworking over 20 years ago, I had no idea it would become part of my healing. I just needed to make something with my hands, and as I built cabinets and carved curves and refined edges, I realized it was not just about the wood, it was about rebuilding myself. Quietly and patiently. God did not show me the whole plan, he seldom does. He just gave me the next step: Pick up the chisel, smooth the edges, and show up. That is how faith works - not in leaps, but in small faithful steps.

Practices to Integrate Faith During the Pivot

If you are looking to make faith a part of your pivot, here are a few grounded practices that helped me and others I know:

1. Start with a Daily Check-In - You do not need an hour or even need a quiet room. Just a few minutes each morning—asking, "What's weighing on me?" "What am I being called to today?" "Where can I let go?" This is prayer. This is alignment. This is spiritual clarity.
2. Surround Yourself with Grounded People - Not perfect people, or performative people, but people who walk in quiet strength. People who show up and remind you of who you are when you forget. Faith grows in community, so find a men's group, a women's circle, a mentor, a friend. Show up with honesty because that is where faith expands.
3. Read Something Anchoring - Be it scripture, devotionals, reflections, or memoirs from people who have walked hard roads and come out the other side, because these stories will feed you when you are running on empty. My go-to book in a dark season? Man's Search for Meaning by Viktor Frankl. It is not a religious book, but it is a deeply spiritual one. One of my favorite, most meaningful parts of the book has Frankl standing in the concentration camp-naked in front of the Nazi captors and he has the realization that while they could take everything from him - clothes, shoes, freedom - they could never take one freedom from him and that was the freedom to CHOOSE how you react to what happens to you.Inspiring. Find what speaks to your soul and return to it often.
4. Create Something - Faith lives in creativity, so build something, write something, paint, plant, volunteer, or serve. Just do some-

thing that puts you back into the act of creation, because that is where you will find a piece of God again.

5. Practice Gratitude, even in the Unknown - Every night, name three things you are thankful for, even if they are small. Especially if they are small because gratitude softens the grip of fear and turns the unknown into sacred space.

Real World Example: Wade Odum: Faith Amid Paralysis

For my good friend and brother, Wade Odum, the pivot wasn't just a shift in career or calling—it was a daily confrontation with the limits of his own body. Wade lives with Hypokalemic Periodic Paralysis (HKPP), a rare and debilitating neuromuscular disorder marked by sudden episodes of full-body weakness or paralysis, brought on by dangerously low potassium levels. At times, his body would betray him completely, collapsing under its own weight, muscles seizing, strength vanishing without warning. Before his diagnosis, the unexplained symptoms created confusion, fear, and frustration, but instead of withdrawing, Wade leaned into his faith and the community around him. A longtime audio engineer and church musician, Wade chose to use his voice—figuratively and literally—to share his experience with grace and clarity. In a March 2024 podcast episode titled In This Body: Living with HKPP through Faith and Love of Family & Community, Wade opened up about his condition, the spiritual journey it catalyzed, and the lessons that suffering had carved into his soul.

His pivot was not just physical; it was deeply internal as living with HKPP required Wade to relinquish control over the parts of life most people take for granted. Each episode of paralysis taught him something new about patience, vulnerability, and trust. The act of surrender became a discipline and dependence on others, once a source of embarrassment, became a wellspring of deeper relationships. And still, Wade remained creative and continued crafting soundscapes for worship services, offering his gifts behind the scenes, where few noticed—but many felt the impact. In his story, we see a quiet form of resilience: the kind that doesn't roar but endures. The kind that says, I will not let this define me, but I will let it shape me.

Wade's pivot wasn't about beating a disease. It was about choosing faith over fear, presence over pity, and purpose even in weakness. In doing so, he reminds us that sometimes the most profound pivots are not the ones we choose—but the ones we faithfully live through.

Wade is one of my oldest friends, going back over 30+ years. We have played music together, roadied for each other, prayed with and for each other and shed tears of sorrow and joy together. Through the sheer tenacity of his wife Carol, she found a vitamin and supplement regime that put his death sentence at bay. Wade is a true inspiration in that, where many would have resigned themselves to that death sentence - he did not. He pivoted. He fought. And he is LIVING. While there are many running around with a heartbeat and breath in their lungs, they are not all living. Wade is - and I am blessed to have him in my life.

Final Thoughts: The Pivot Is Holy Ground

You may not feel it now and you may feel broken or lost or unsure, but I need you to hear this: This season? This messy, in-between, identity-shifting season? It is holy ground. This is where you meet yourself again and this is where you meet God again. This is where everything you have been through starts to make sense—not all at once, but piece by piece, so let faith lead you, even if all you have is a whisper of direction. Trust that there is more ahead than behind and that you are not alone.

Trust that your life still matters—even when it looks different than you planned, because the pivot is not the end. It is the beginning of something sacred.

Keep walking.

📔 Reflection & Action

1. What part of this chapter resonated with you most? Why?
2. What is one action you can take this week to apply a principle discussed here?
3. Are there any habits or beliefs you need to let go of to pivot successfully?
4. Who can you talk to for support or accountability around this pivot?

18. Finding Purpose Through Service: The Power of Service Before Self

Some folks spend a lifetime trying to find their purpose like it's buried treasure—something hidden far off in the future, waiting to be uncovered through enough self-discovery, journaling, or soul-searching retreats. But here's what life—and almost three decades in a uniform—has taught me: purpose isn't something you find at the top of the mountain; it's something you uncover at the feet of others when you kneel to serve. I've seen grown men fall apart because their careers ended too soon, and I've watched bright young women burn out chasing titles and degrees they didn't even want. I've seen addicts, convicts, widows, and wounded warriors turn their entire lives around not because they "found themselves," but because they started showing up for someone else. That's where it turns - that's where it pivots and when the center of gravity shifts away from me and toward us.

The Heartbeat of Service

The most effective teams I have been part of—including SWAT, M.A.I.T., narcotics units, and the auto theft task force—were founded on a fundamental principle: prioritizing service above personal interest. That wasn't just something we said when it looked good on a plaque, it was how we moved, how we made decisions and it meant that when the call came in at 3:00 a.m., you didn't think about how tired you were or how much paperwork was waiting on your desk. You thought about the family trapped in that car, you thought about the kid lost in those woods, or you thought about whatever it was someone else needed—and you moved. Here's the secret they don't teach you in school: that way of life isn't just for police officers or soldiers or firefighters. It's for anyone willing to stop asking, "What do I want from this life?" and start asking, "What does this life need from me?"

Scars as Service

You don't have to be perfect to serve. In fact, some of the most impactful people I know carry deep scars, and that's exactly what qualifies them. I think about a woman I knew, Lisa, who lost her teenage son in a DUI crash and for two or three years, she went dark. She couldn't get out of bed, couldn't speak his name, and did not know how to go on, but eventually, through the help of a small church group and a counselor who had walked a similar road, she found Mothers Against Drunk Driving and she started volunteering—first with a grief support hotline, then eventually speaking at high schools about drunk driving. She told me once, "I thought I'd never stop drowning in pain, but when I started helping other people keep their kids safe, it didn't take the pain away—but it gave my pain a purpose."

That's it. That's the heart of the pivot. Turning what broke you into what builds others, and in the process, you start to become whole again.

Purpose Is Found, Not Fabricated

The world will try to sell you a version of purpose that looks like achievement, whether it is a six-figure job, a social media platform, or a TED Talk. There is nothing wrong with any of that, but that is not purpose. The kind of purpose that anchors you in a storm—the kind that lasts when the money dries up or the applause fades—is almost always rooted in service. If you ask the happiest people you know—really ask them— about their purpose or what drives them, you'll usually hear something simple: "I mentor young men coming out of the foster system." "I started cooking for the homeless once a week." "I take care of my neighbor's kid while she works two jobs." These aren't grand gestures, but they are consistent, intentional acts of showing up and they breathe life into the people who give as much as the people who receive.

Service Rewires Your Brain

You don't have to take my word for it—science backs this up, as there are studies showing that serving others can reduce symptoms of depression, increase feelings of meaning and connection, and even improve your physical health. When you get outside yourself, when you stop spinning in your own head, you create space for something better to take root: gratitude, resilience, and clarity. And let's be honest—when you're in the middle of a life pivot, clarity is one of the hardest things to come by. Look, here it is: if you feel stuck, serve. Volunteer. Help a neighbor move. Coach Little League. Visit a nursing home. It doesn't matter how big or small the act is—what matters is that you move your focus from internal to external, from "What am I missing?" to "How can I help?" It is almost miraculous how fast purpose starts to appear when you start giving of yourself.

Legacy Over Lifestyle

One of my old supervisors, mentor, and friend, Paul Wing, once told me after he went through a dark period where the politics of the department came after him unjustly, "Don't chase lifestyle—build legacy." That has always stuck with me. Many people pivot because they think the next chapter will make them happier, richer, or more admired, but if you ask people at the end of their life what they're most proud of, they rarely talk about jobs or status. What they talk about is people and about the lives they touched, about the kids they mentored, the marriage they fought for, the family they raised, and the community they showed up for. Legacy is built in the quiet moments of service, not in front of a camera, but behind the scenes and not in your resume, but in someone else's story of healing or hope.

Start Where You Are

You don't have to be in a position of power to have influence, because some of the greatest shifts I've seen come from ordinary people doing extraordinary things—simply because they chose to. It is not about position, power, or status - it is about being willing to give. You don't need a degree in social work to sit with someone in pain and you certainly don't need to be a millionaire to bring a warm meal to a family going through it. Trust me, you don't need to have all your own pieces put together to start helping someone else pick theirs up, because all you need is a willing heart and a bit of courage and it may even pay bigger rewards for your soul than those you are serving.

Real World Example: Rand Padgett (Retired - finally)

For Rand Padgett, life's most defining moments have come not just through crisis or hardship, but also through unexpected opportunities— each one met with the quiet grit passed down from generations of hardworking farmers. Raised with a strong moral compass and an unwavering commitment to effort, integrity, and perseverance, Rand's pivots have never been random. They were always directed by faith, character, and a belief in leaving people better than he found them.

Rand's first major pivot came as a young music student, driven by a deep love of performance. After touring Europe with a high school orchestra and pursuing a music major in college, his dream of becoming a band director met a hard truth: he lacked the necessary piano skills. Devastated but determined, he re-calibrated. With the help of a guidance counselor, Rand pivoted toward law enforcement, earning degrees in Police Science and Criminology. This early course correction became the foundation for a long and meaningful career in public service. Though raised in a Protestant home, Rand's spiritual journey took a new path after marrying his wife and becoming a father to her two young children. Invited to attend her church, he ultimately converted to the Church of Jesus Christ of Latter-day Saints. This shift not only deepened his faith but also introduced a lifestyle of health and discipline that he credits with preserving his well-being for over four decades. Spiritual growth and personal transformation became guiding forces in the chapters that have come since.

After retiring from a distinguished 30-year law enforcement career in California, Rand and his wife moved to a rural town—seeking peace and purpose. Instead, they met hostility and rejection from the local community and despite his experience, he was turned away from job after job. The closed doors led to an extraordinary window: a contract role embedded with the U.S. Army in Afghanistan. Rand served with front-line units, took part in over 200 missions, and later trained police forces in Pakistan, Tanzania, and other global hot spots through the Department of Justice. A season of rejection became one of the most adventurous and impactful chapters of his life. When international contracts slowed, Rand pivoted again—this time into the National Park Service as a Seasonal Law Enforcement Ranger at age 60. The work was physically and emotionally demanding, and during this time, he faced the unbearable grief of losing his 35-year-old daughter, Laura, to cancer. This profound personal loss reshaped his perspective on time, legacy, and the importance of presence.

While finishing he's tenure as a park ranger, Rand was invited to apply for a position as a Criminal Justice Academy Director and Department Chair at a California community college. He seized the opportunity and began leading the kind of academy where he once taught as adjunct faculty. Over the course of the next six years, Rand grew the department, mentored new generations of law enforcement professionals, and fulfilled a dream he never thought would resurface. Rand is not done either. He still has a mission and a purpose. He gardens with his wife, Carol, he volunteers at his Church helping with those who have various addictions, he trains others in marksmanship and firearms safety, and spends time with his family and grandchildren.

Rand's life proves that pivots are less about abandoning a path and more about realigning with purpose. Whether in a band uniform, body armor, or a classroom, Rand responded to change with humility and resolve. His story is proof that when you engage fully—mentally, spiritually, and physically—good things eventually follow. I was blessed to work for Rand as his academy coordinator and got to see up close and personal the concepts we will be discussing throughout this book. Love, faith, integrity, resilience- all these traits got Rand through life and into his golden years. More importantly, during all his pivots he shared and showed these traits with those around him in his service to others.

At the heart of every pivot Rand made was a simple, powerful belief: we all have more capacity than we think. It is only by testing the boundaries of our faith, resilience, and character that we discover what's truly possible. And when we commit ourselves to worthy causes, we do more than succeed—we thrive.

Final Thought: Let Service Lead the Pivot

If you're in the middle of a life pivot—confused, tired, searching— here's my challenge to you: Let service lead the way and ask yourself: Who around me is hurting right now? What burden could I lighten today? What have I survived that someone else might still be walking through? Then move. Not someday, not when you have it all figured out, but today. Right now, in whatever way you can, because at the end of the day, "service before self" isn't just a code for first responders. It is a compass for anyone trying to live a life that matters and when you live that way—when you serve before you seek—you'll often find that purpose was waiting for you there all along.

Reflection Questions: Who in your life right now might need what you have to offer—your time, your story, your encouragement? When have you felt most alive, most useful, most like yourself? What were you doing? Who were you helping? What would change if you stopped asking "What's my purpose?" and started asking "Who can I serve today?"

📓 Reflection & Action

1. What part of this chapter resonated with you most? Why?
2. What is one action you can take this week to apply a principle discussed here?

3. Are there any habits or beliefs you need to let go of to pivot successfully?

4. Who can you talk to for support or accountability around this pivot?

19

19. When the Pivot Is Forced on You: Grief, Loss, and What Comes Next

The Day It All Changed

There's a kind of pivot you don't choose, and it doesn't come after reflection or strategy. It comes like a wrecking ball through your living room window, it doesn't knock politely, and it doesn't wait until you're ready. It occurs rapidly and unexpectedly, leaving individuals unprepared and without guidance on how to continue. I've seen a lot of death in my line of work and some of that is the nature of law enforcement — you show up after the worst thing has already happened. But there are some losses that don't just happen around you because they happen *to* you. They crawl inside your chest and stay awhile.

Now, I was never close to any of my grandparents, because they lived out of state and rarely visited, and my parents and siblings are all still alive, so the first time I got that kind of call that hit so personally was February 13, 2013. A rogue LAPD officer had gone on a killing rampage and had hidden out in the San Bernardino County mountains. He finally popped out and the chase was on, and my whole narcotics team, SWAT, and everyone else was on their way. When I was about 4 minutes away from the location, the call went out for an officer down. That officer turned out to be a friend, Jeremiah Mackay. Jeremiah was a diamond of a human being and that proverbial guy that would do anything for anyone and give you the shirt right off their back. It has stayed with me for a long time and still takes up space in my head that, "what would have happened if I had been quicker." The reality is I may have been shot too, like another of our guys, Alex Collins – but the mind still plays those games with you. I think about Jeremiah every day.

Afterward, the world didn't make sense for a long time, it was like someone had taken all the furniture out of my house while I was gone and I kept bumping into walls that weren't supposed to be there, because grief does that. It rearranges the entire layout of your life and it makes no sense. That's why this chapter matters, because many of you did not get the chance to *choose* your pivot. It was forced on you — by death, by divorce, by betrayal, by life just being unfair, and now you're trying to figure out who you are *after.*

So, let's talk about it. Honestly and quietly with no motivational quotes or clichés, just truth.

What Grief Actually Feels Like

While grief does not look the same for everyone, there are some common themes. Grief is not tidy, and it doesn't move in a straight line from denial to acceptance like they say in the textbooks. At times, you may feel well, but unexpectedly, a certain scent, piece of music, or a handwritten note can evoke a strong emotional response. It's a physical thing and you can feel it in your chest, behind your eyes, and in your throat. It makes time feel slippery and you forget how to do simple things, you feel guilty for laughing, you feel angry when people say the wrong thing, or you want to be left alone — and also desperately want someone to sit with you and not say a word.

Grief, real grief, is the realization that things will never go back to the way they were — and your mind is trying everything it can to argue with that fact.

That's the first truth: **Grief is not a problem to be solved; it is a condition to be lived through.**

Loss Changes You

The truth is that you will not "just get over it." That's not how loss works, because you do not return to who you were before. That person's gone and you *become* someone new — someone who now carries this scar, this silence, and this memory stitched into the fabric of who you are. And that's not all bad.

While we live in a culture that treats pain like a detour, the fact of the matter is that pain *is* the road sometimes and not the detour. Grief opens a part of you that comfort never could, and it makes you pay attention. It slows you down and shows you what really matters — and who really matters. You may be softer now, or harder and you may trust less or forgive faster, or you may cry more easily or never cry again. These are not flaws, they are markers of what you've lived through and here's the pivot: you get to decide what kind of person you become *after* the loss. You may not have had a choice in what happened, but you have every bit of say in how you respond to it. That response is the pivot.

The Temptations After Loss

After a major loss, we're vulnerable — physically, emotionally, and spiritually. and when we're vulnerable, there are some tempting shortcuts that look like healing, but aren't. Let me call out a few I have seen in myself and in others:

1. Numbing Out - This one's popular. It could be alcohol or drugs, scrolling, work, or even religion if used like a sedative instead of a balm. It could be anything you use to avoid feeling, but feelings don't disappear when you ignore them. They just wait, and trust me, they will surface when you least expect — and often in ways that hurt others.

2. Rush to Move On - Society loves resilience stories, and you will often hear things like: "Look how fast they bounced back." But grief doesn't care about optics and if you rush the healing, you risk building on a cracked foundation. It's okay to sit in the ashes a while because that doesn't make you weak, it makes you *real*.

3. Clinging to the Past - There's comfort in holding on — to their clothes, their routines, the way life *was*, but sometimes, holding on too tight keeps you from reaching out. You're not dishonoring someone by living, you honor them by becoming someone who carries their memory with courage.

4. Isolation - Grief makes you feel like no one understands, and while that might be true — no one had *your* loss - there are people who know what it's like to lose, to ache, to wonder if life can ever feel normal again, so let them in.

How You Find Your Bearings Again

Healing doesn't look like a Hollywood movie and there is no big moment where the music swells and everything makes sense. It's quiet, unseen, and incremental.

· You get up one morning and make coffee. You didn't want to, but you did.

- You laugh at something on accident. Then feel guilty and then realize that laughter doesn't betray the one you lost — it's a sign you're still here.
- You go back to the gym, or the trail, or the garage - just something that reminds your body that it can still move forward.
- You answer the phone. Not just texts. You talk.
- You stop apologizing for how long it's taking.

And one day — not all at once, but gradually — you start to believe that your life still has meaning, even without the person or season or identity you lost.

You're Not the Only One

Remember, you are not alone in this. While it seems like you are the first one to experience loss, everyone has experienced some kind of loss – it is different for everyone, but it is loss. I am here, still carrying the loss of my brothers like a folded flag on my chest, but in a lot of ways, I think I have been able to use that ache to show up differently — for my family, my coworkers, for every kid I've ever had to tell, "I'm sorry, he's gone."

You are not the only one who has had to rebuild, and you are not the only one who has had to pivot through pain. You are in good company.

Finding Your Footing After Loss

You didn't ask for this, but you *are* here and that matters. This isn't a checklist. It's a conversation. Quiet, slow, honest.

The GRIT Grid: Four Coordinates for Grieving

| **G** – *Grounded in Reality* | What am I pretending didn't happen? What truth am I avoiding? |

| **R** – *Reclaiming Routine* | What simple action keeps me tethered to life? |

| **I** – *Integrating the Memory* | How do I want to honor what I lost — not avoid it? |

| **T** – *Turning Toward the Future* | What might I be ready for now, even in a small way? |

- Write a letter to the person you lost. Or to yourself.
- Name one way you're different since the loss. Don't judge it.
- Share your story with someone who can handle the weight.
- Light a candle. Sit quietly. Say their name.

Real Life Example: Alex Maddox - Widow / Survivor of a Hero / Speaker / Role Model

I met Alex Maddox through the Cannonball Memorial Run, when we honored her husband, Patrolman Chase Lee Maddox of the Locust Grove Police Department. I remember standing there, surrounded by the weight of that moment, looking at a young widow who carried herself with a quiet strength that stopped me in my tracks. Her life had been split into two parts— "before" and "after"—but what struck me was how fiercely determined she was to build something meaningful in the "after." Alex's story isn't just about surviving loss; it's about refusing to let tragedy define you.

Her husband Chase, the love of her life, was the kind of man who believed in service, and showed up for his community every single day.

On February 9, 2018, he was killed in the line of duty—a moment that forever altered Alex's world. She was nine months pregnant at the time, and just four days after losing her husband, she gave birth to their son, Bodie. Their older son, Bradin, was already facing his own challenges with a congenital brain malformation and on October 25, 2022, Bradin also went home to be with the Lord and his dad. It would have been easy for Alex to crumble under the weight of it all, but she didn't and Alex turned her grief into a mission. She co-founded Chase It Up, a foundation that sends new recruits through the police academy each year—continuing Chase's calling even though he's no longer here to see it. She also took on a leadership role as President of the Georgia Chapter of Band of Blue, supporting families of fallen officers with a depth of understanding only someone who has lived that pain can offer.

Through the Folds of Honor scholarship program, Alex is pursuing a communications degree to better mentor and guide other widows who find themselves at the same crossroads she once faced. She is also a national speaker for Folds of Honor, honoring Chase's memory continually. She even carries a tattoo of the sound wave of Chase's voice saying "I love you," a daily reminder that love doesn't end when life changes—it transforms into the fire that pushes you forward. And Alex has found love again - she is not just surviving, she is thriving - because she pivoted and refused to accept defeat. She knew she had a bigger calling in this life and she has stepped into the gap to live that calling, while still honoring the memory of her late husband and son. Alex is a huge inspiration to me, and should be to everyone.

Her story is a living example of what it means to pivot: when life breaks you, you can stay shattered, or you can build something unshakable out of the pieces. Alex chose to build.

Final Word

If this chapter stirred something in you — sadness, regret, even anger — that's okay, because that means you're still breathing, still feeling, and still fighting. While you may never fully move on, you *can* move forward even if it's slow and even if it's in boots filled with tears.

And that, my friend, is a pivot worth honoring.

📖 Reflection & Action

1. What part of this chapter resonated with you most? Why?
2. What is one action you can take this week to apply a principle discussed here?
3. Are there any habits or beliefs you need to let go of to pivot successfully?
4. Who can you talk to for support or accountability around this pivot?

VII

Part Seven

Case Studies and Closing Thoughts

20

Conclusion

The Journey of the Pivot — Finding Your Way Forward

If there is a single concept I hope you retain upon concluding this book, it is that change is not merely an inevitable aspect of life—it also represents one of its most significant opportunities. Life is not a straight path, it is a series of turns, detours, and sometimes full stops that demand we pivot — to adjust, to rethink, to reinvent and while these moments of change can feel like storms shaking us to the core, they also open the door to something remarkable: the chance to live with more honesty, more purpose, and more alignment with who we really are.

The road through a pivot is never a smooth one. It is often messy and confusing, filled with doubt and fear, but it is also the road where courage is forged and resilience grows. The journey asks us to show up — sometimes when all we want to do is run away and it asks us to trust in ourselves and in the process, even when the path ahead is foggy and uncertain.

Over the course of this book, we have explored what it means to recognize when it is time to pivot, how to learn from setbacks without losing heart, and how to manage the practical realities like money and relationships as you navigate change. We talked about the importance of honest communication — with others, but also with yourself. We dug into the idea that waiting for perfect clarity is often just a way to stay stuck, and that movement — even imperfect movement — is the key to finding your way forward.

As we come to the end, I want to gather those pieces into a bigger picture — not as a set of rules, but as a way of living through change with strength and grace. A pivot is not a single moment — it is a process, sometimes slow and uneven. It is not about one big breakthrough that fixes everything all at once, as growth rarely looks that neat or tidy. More often, it is messy. You take one step, then stumble. You try again, and sometimes it feels like you are moving backwards, but every time you get up, you gain strength. You learn a little more about who you are and what you need.

Life does not move in a straight line, and your pivot will not either and will be fits and starts, times when you want to quit, and times when you surprise yourself with how far you have come. It is a journey that asks for patience — with yourself and with the process.

If there is one lesson I learned as a law enforcement officer, it is this: hesitation in the face of danger can be deadly. On the street, waiting to be sure can mean getting caught in the worst possible spot and the same holds true in life. Momentum, not perfection, is what keeps you alive — and what moves you forward. You do not have to walk this path alone. In fact, you should not. Change touches every part of your life — your identity, your relationships, your sense of purpose — and the people you surround yourself with will make all the difference. Your circle, the people who walk with you, who tell you the hard truths, who hold space for your fear and your dreams — those are the ones you want nearby. Building that circle means choosing people who encourage you to be better, who see your potential even when you do not, and who support you without enabling excuses. It also means letting go — with kindness and grace — of those who drain your energy or hold you back. Setting boundaries is not about pushing people away; it is about making room for what truly matters.

Courage shows up repeatedly throughout this journey. Courage is not the absence of fear, it is acting despite fear — speaking hard truths, stepping into the unknown, choosing to move forward even when the ground feels shaky beneath your feet.

When I told my wife I was stepping away from my career in law enforcement, it was one of the hardest decisions I ever had. The fear was real, because the unknown was terrifying, but it was that moment of courage — saying the truth aloud — that began to shift everything. It turned the storm inside my head into something my wife and I could face together. Courage grows with practice and every time you choose to take a step forward, even when your hands shake, you build strength and you remind yourself that fear does not have to be a stop sign — it can be a signal to move forward anyway.

So often, we think we need to have it all figured out before we start moving, but that is just not how it works. Clarity comes after movement and the path becomes clearer as you begin to walk it. One step reveals the next. One conversation opens the door to the next. I have seen people wait for the "right time" for years — afraid to act because they did not have all the answers or because they feared failure, but time does not wait. Life keeps moving whether we are ready or not and while waiting often feels safe, it is really a form of paralysis.

Taking that first step — making the call, starting the conversation, changing the routine — even when you do not have it all figured out, is what changes lives.

Movement creates momentum.

Momentum brings clarity.

Setbacks will come, and when they do, do not mistake them for failure. Setbacks are lessons disguised in challenging times. They test you, yes, but they also teach you. They show you what is working and what is not, and they reveal where you need to adjust course. When your plans fall apart, lean into the lessons, because those who persevere do not let setbacks define them — they let setbacks refine them.

Through it all, your well-being is the foundation you build on and it is easy to neglect your health — mental, emotional, physical — when everything is shaking. But without a solid foundation, the weight of change becomes too heavy, so protect your well-being fiercely. Rest, eat well, move your body, and seek support, because taking care of yourself is not selfish; it is necessary for the journey.

Financial uncertainty can feel like a mountain blocking your path, but with honest assessment and smart planning, you can build stability step by step. Freedom comes when you manage your money wisely instead of letting it control you and facing financial realities head-on may be uncomfortable, but it is one of the most empowering things you can do in a pivot.

And do not forget the power of honest communication. Change stretches relationships in ways you cannot always predict, so speaking your truth — early, clearly, and respectfully — builds bridges. It creates alignment. It lets others walk with you, rather than leaving you to carry the weight alone.

You will have to make tough decisions and act on them, so stop waiting for the perfect moment that does not exist. The life you want is waiting on the other side of action, not thought or fear. Every pivot is built from countless small decisions, each one moving you closer to who you are meant to become.

This journey will not be easy, but it will be worth it. Every step you take, every hard conversation you have, every fear you face will bring you closer to a life that feels true. You will discover strength you did not know you had, and a freedom that comes only from showing up fully and moving forward — even when you are scared. Your story is still being written and the chapters ahead will hold more change, more challenges, and more growth, but each pivot builds on the last, shaping you into someone stronger and more aligned.

Walk this path with faith — faith in yourself, in the process, and in something bigger — even when you do not see the whole way ahead. Courage is not about never being afraid; it is about choosing to move forward despite the fear.

Keep your eyes on the horizon and look beyond the doubts, the pain, the confusion. See the life you are building and lean into that vision. Let it guide you when the road gets dark, because change is hard, but you are harder. You were built for this and you have the strength, the wisdom, and the resilience to pivot and rise.

You are not alone, you are not stuck, and you are on the move, so lean into your pivot. Walk through the fire and speak your truth. Build your circle and take the first step. Keep moving forward, because the life you want — the life you were made for — is waiting.

And that journey starts now.

Your Next Steps: A Call to Action

Now, as you close this book, I want to offer you some invitations — not just ideas to think about, but actions to take.

First, take a moment to pause and reflect honestly: Where are you on your pivot journey? Are you still circling the runway, stuck in fear or uncertainty? Or are you ready to take the next step forward, even if it is small?

Write it down. Name it. Speak it aloud. Clarity begins with honest acknowledgment.

Next, find one action you can take today that moves you forward. It does not have to be a giant leap, it might be a phone call you have been avoiding, a conversation you need to have, or simply setting a goal for the week. Whatever it is, commit to doing it before this day ends.

Reach out to someone who can walk with you — a friend, a mentor, a family member and tell them where you are. Ask for their support or simply invite them to listen. Remember, you do not have to do this alone.

Begin building or reshaping your circle intentionally and look for those who challenge and encourage you. Give yourself permission to set boundaries with those who drain your energy or doubt your dreams and take care of yourself fiercely. Prioritize your physical, emotional, and mental health because small habits build big strength over time.

Finally, remember to speak your truth. Practice courageous communication — with yourself and with others because it is the bridge to alignment and the foundation for sustainable change.

Your pivot is not a one-time event; it is a living process. You will stumble. You will learn. And you will grow, and if you keep moving — one step, one breath at a time — you will find your way.

I want to leave you with this: Your life is waiting on the other side of action. The freedom, the peace, the purpose you seek are within reach. You have everything it takes to pivot and rise. So, take the first step. Then take the next.

Keep moving forward because your best life is ahead of you.

A Request for all of You

As we close this out, I have a couple things I want you to think about - for yourself and anyone you know who may be going through a pivot......

1. Life is not binary. I once had a SWAT commander say that you are either and asset or a liability. This may hold true in a very limited field on a limited basis, but it is a very dangerous way to think of life, because there is always, at least, a third option. Life is rarely as simple as labeling someone an asset or a liability as

we are not fixed values on a balance sheet, defined by what we give or take in a single moment. A person can be both — capable of great contributions while also carrying struggles or challenges that require support. Growth, healing, and purpose all happen in the messy middle, where people can evolve, adapt, and learn from both their strengths and their shortcomings. To reduce someone to either "useful" or "burdensome" ignores the complexity of being human. Life is not binary; it is fluid, and the roles we play shift with time, circumstances, and perspective.

2. Check in on your brothers and sisters. When our time in our field comes to an end, there can be extreme isolation - and that too is very dangerous because if we don't have the right self talk, we can end up on the floor in the closet with a pistol. One of the most dangerous things after a major pivot—whether it's leaving the job, retiring, or stepping away from a life you've always known— is isolation. When the noise fades and the structure disappears, the silence can get loud. That's when the demons show up—the doubts, the "what ifs," the regrets. Too many good men and women get lost there because they don't have anyone pulling them back into the fight. This is why checking up on your brothers matters. A simple call, a text, a coffee—those small acts can be a lifeline, and we need to remind each other that we're still in this together, that our worth isn't tied to the last badge we wore or the last mission we ran, or the last sale we made. Brotherhood doesn't end when the pivot comes; if anything, that's when it matters most.

Let's go!

Cheers, James.

About the Author

Author Bio – James Snow

James Snow is a retired Sergeant from the San Bernardino County Sheriff's Department, where he served for nearly three decades in a wide range of roles, including SWAT sniper, narcotics investigator, traffic division supervisor, and Major Accident Investigation Team (M.A.I.T.) leader. Known for his deep expertise in vehicle collision reconstruction, public safety leadership, and tactical operations, James developed a reputation as both a decisive operator and a thoughtful educator.

Throughout his law enforcement career, James trained hundreds of officers as a POST-certified instructor and academy coordinator. He developed and led instructional programs in traffic collision analysis, corrections, tactical response, and leadership. His commitment to education extended beyond the badge, serving as an adjunct professor at Victor Valley College and Park University, where he taught courses in criminal justice, forensic science, and the administration of justice.

After retiring from active duty, James channeled his creative energy into woodworking and storytelling. He co-founded a custom woodworking business dedicated to the timeless craftsmanship of the Greene and Greene tradition, producing heirloom-quality pieces built with precision and purpose. His work in the trades has been featured nationally, including multiple guest appearances on the television series *Restored*, where he brought his technical skill and design sensibility to historic renovation projects.

James also serves as a proud board member of the Cannonball Memorial Run, a 501(c)(3) nonprofit organization dedicated to honoring fallen law enforcement officers and supporting their surviving families. His commitment to service did not end with his career—it evolved into new forms of leadership and mentorship.

As an author, James brings the full weight of his life experience to the page. His book, *The Pivot*, blends hard-earned wisdom, personal reflection, and practical tools to help others navigate life's inevitable turning points. Whether in the courtroom, the classroom, the wood shop, or the written word, James Snow remains committed to building things that last—especially lives anchored in resilience, character, and meaning.